September 2016
for Clea with love
Jane + Vincent

LUMITECTURE

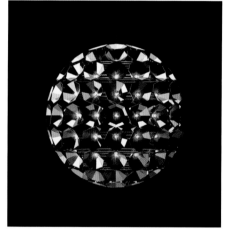

ANNA YUDINA

LUMI TECTURE

ILLUMINATING INTERIORS
FOR DESIGNERS & ARCHITECTS

Thames & Hudson

CONTENTS

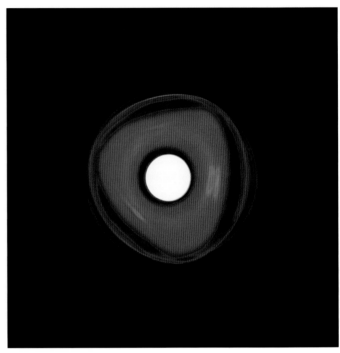

TRANSFORMING TIME __ 108

TRANSFORMING EMOTION __ 164

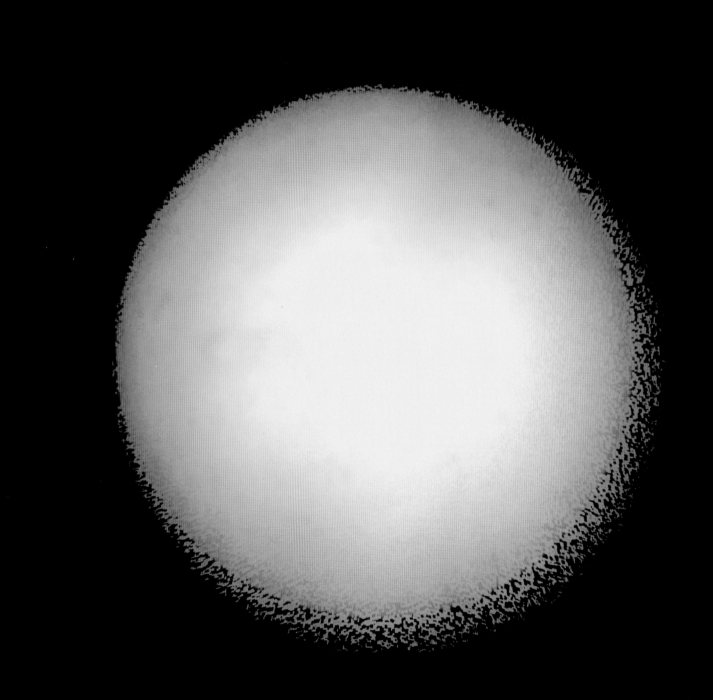

INTRODUCTION

LIGHT

What is light? Is it a source, a tool or an experience? Our emotional response to a room after turning on a switch may be just a small part of the answer, yet it already shows that light is all of the above, and more.

'Architecture creates a space where there was none,' notes architect Peter Zumthor. 'At the beginning, the space is completely dark, and then you start slowly opening it. This element is inherent to imagining a space: you think about the amount of light you need, and where and what this light should do.' »

What this light does – in a space or to a space – is the theme at the heart of this book. But is it only space that is affected when light appears out of the darkness? Does light influence the way we experience architecture, for example? In the 1950s, lighting expert Richard Kelly famously coined the terms 'focal glow', 'ambient luminescence' and 'play of brilliants' to make sense of these questions. Light makes an architectural space liveable, shapes it and guides us through it, yet the power of light reaches beyond a response to purely pragmatic needs.

Perhaps my most revelatory encounter with light happened in Norway, while visiting one of the country's best-known natural attractions, the serpentine mountain road of Trollstigen. The road's eleven hairpin bends were bathed in thick fog, as was our eventual destination – the beautifully cantilevered observation deck, with its picture-postcard view practically obliterated. What I got instead was bigger: a uniform, shining whiteness, which radiated power and sounded like a waterfall.

The experience I had on that day has echoes of the work of American light artist Doug Wheeler, who uses light to design white, shadowless and seemingly borderless spaces in an attempt to 'create absence', as well as of James Turrell, who explores the 'thingness' of light. In Turrell's artwork, light appears as a physical presence and is able to generate or erase boundaries and entire spatial dimensions. Between 'absence' and 'thingness' exists a vast realm of possibilities in transforming space through light.

Light supports and shapes our daily schedules; turns an oppressive room without a view into one of elegant serenity; comforts and disturbs; relaxes and energizes; conceals and reveals. It can also challenge our ideas about the physical reality. The Dutch artist Matthijs Munnik plays with frequencies of stroboscopic light to create hallucinatory effects and reveal some of the workings of our visual process. 'Using light in an extraordinary way leads to extraordinary perceptions,' he says. 'With light as a medium, I can explore the fringes of our perception.'

The evolutionary leap in lighting technology has produced objects that are ever-more compact, flexible and efficient, releasing unprecedented potential in rethinking the architecture we live in.

D-N SF 12 PG VI 14, DOUG WHEELER
A SENSE OF INFINITY CREATED WITH THE HELP OF DMX-CONTROLLED
LED LIGHTS, REINFORCED FIBREGLASS AND TITANIUM DIOXIDE PAINT

Apart from the development of newer and better light sources, other, less obvious factors are also at work.

In an interview with *Uncube* magazine, Kjetil Trædal Thorsen, co-founder of architectural firm Snøhetta, points out one such indirect influence: the practice of using laptops and mobile phones as sources of light. In it, he noted: 'One of the first apps converted your mobile phone into a torch, which represents the individualization of light, carried close to your body, from one space to another. It's a bit like it was before electricity was introduced, when you carried a moveable lamp around with you from room to room. So the lit surface is reduced to only that which you need to get information from, and the rest of the space around you can remain dark – reducing energy use, too.'

As a result, general and task lighting merge and become an extension of our bodies, rather than part of the interior design. Architect Philippe Rahm (pp. 70–3, 152–3, 204–5, 247) also uses the different properties of light – such as its colour, or the heat released by various types of light sources – as the parameters that add 'physiological' and 'meteorological' dimensions to our habitual interior layouts (Domestic Astronomy; pp. 72–3).

Light as a building material must be used mindfully, even sparingly. 'By appreciating the darkness when you design the light,' explains lighting designer Rogier van der Heide, 'you create much more interesting environments that truly enhance our lives.'

As a boy, designer Michael Anastassiades (pp. 59, 170, 255) would visit an architect friend of his father's. Perplexed by the fact that this friend's house was dimly lit in the evenings, it was explained that the difference between day and night existed for a reason, and that there was no need to turn one into the other. Today, Anastassiades still remembers these words when producing his own lighting designs in the search 'for the perfect glow'.

Lighting's effect is such that two different lighting schemes can alter our impression of the same space from chaos to calm at the flick of a switch. The countless factors that define space, light and our relationship to them will only be added by each new creator that joins the conversation.

SOURCING AND ENHANCING LIGHT (CLOCKWISE, FROM TOP LEFT):
HOPE, FRANCISCO GOMEZ PAZ AND PAOLO RIZZATTO (P. 39)
HABATAKI, TAKRAM DESIGN ENGINEERING FOR KONICA MINOLTA
BIO-LIGHT, VHM, PETER GAL AND CEDRIC BERNARD FOR PHILIPS DESIGN
PROBES
ATMOS, FROM THE WATER LAMPS SERIES, ARTURO ERBSMAN (P. 138)

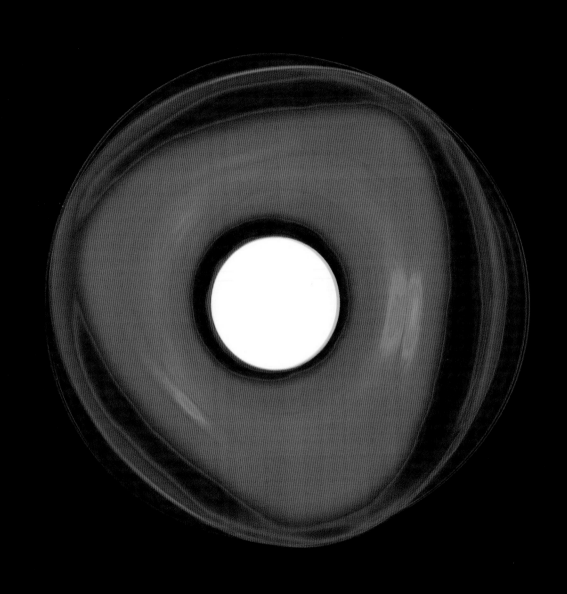

TRANSFORMING

SPACE

Light is the essential ingredient in transforming darkness into a habitable space. This chapter – 'Transforming Space' – is concerned with light as a means of making sense of a space, of enabling its form and function.

The first section, 'Activation', presents light as an accent that can jazz up neutral spaces. This can be achieved by adding an element of surprise, as in the wirelessly powered fluorescent tubes by Brian Richer (p. 31), or in a skeletal design by Rossi Bianchi Lighting Design (p. 27), which seems to contain a light-emitting void. Incorporating extra functions is another option, as seen in Alex Schulz's wardrobe/floor-lamp crossover (p. 32) or Johanna Jacobson Backman's Block, a fusion of office lighting with acoustic panelling (p. 22).

Occasionally, the magic touch arrives as a consequence of budget or structural constraints, as is the case with Mobile Lamp, by Nathalie Dewez (pp. 20–1), an inflatable, oversized luminaire designed for the glazed ceiling of a museum, and the constellation of tiny downlit greenhouses used by Oki Sato of Nendo to display craft objects (pp. 28–9).

From here, it's one step to 'Systems', a section that focuses on modular designs. These designs maximize light output, while minimizing the amount of illuminants, and combine various types of light sources to create multipurpose fixtures, while forming different kinds of nearly architectural configurations that range from practical to dazzling – and are sometimes both.

'Sculpting Space' demonstrates out-of-the-box ideas that illustrate in built form Le Corbusier's definition of the role of lighting in architecture. These lantern walls, luminous domes, landscape-like formations, even three-dimensional cabling, all 'create ambience and the feel of a place, as well as the expression of a structure that houses the functions within it and around it.'

Most of the projects featured in 'Orientation' make use of light as a navigation tool, but – more importantly – they are also an invitation to embrace a space in a more than purely practical sense. They range from a luminous stripe hovering above a huge table in an otherwise dark dining room, to an artwork in which a crisscross of laser beams appears meaningless from all angles except one, to a light-and-colour code that guides art-school students within the building and encourages them to explore the fine line between reality and illusion. Concepts differ, yet in each light is intended to make people not only aware, but also conscious of the surrounding space.

Finally, in 'Materialization', the role of light evolves from modelling a space through highlighting volumes and textures to being used as a building material. We switch between light-transmitting concrete and light-emitting glass panels, see how light reflects off nylon strings to mark the borders of an auditorium, and end up with light projections that become walls, arcades and three-dimensional enclosures – so 'solid' that people can't help touching them, and so ephemeral that their hands pass through these vibrant, luminous veils. From dematerializing matter that seems to lose its weight, thanks to optic fibres or UV-radiating gas, to materializing light, as in the luminous 'structures' of Troika (pp. 102–3) or Anthony McCall (pp. 100–1), in which drawing and sculpture, stillness and motion, 2D and 3D merge into one tactile whole.

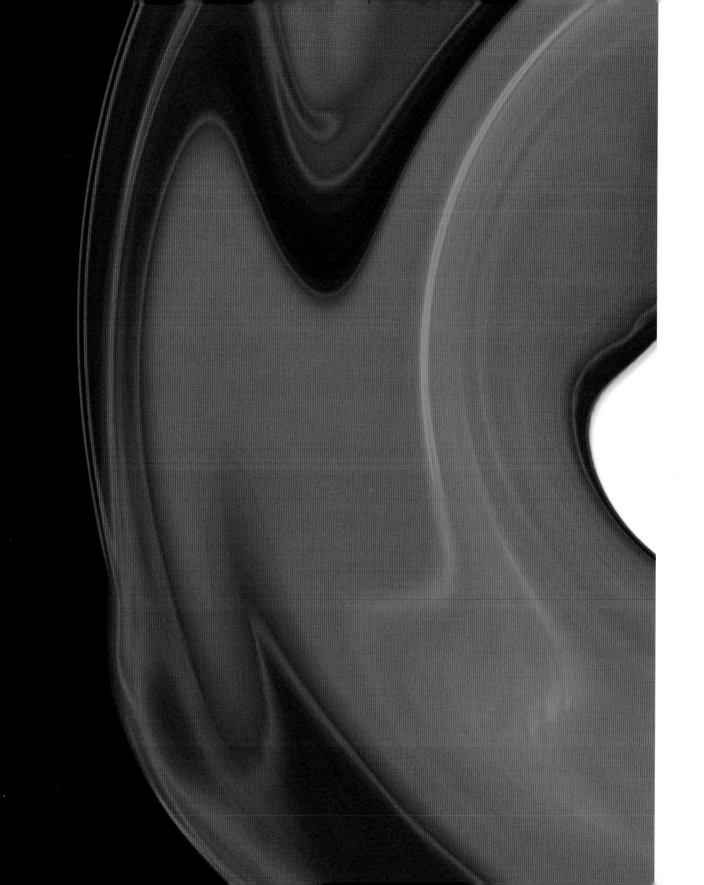

LIGHT OBJECTS 001, 004, 006

NAAMA HOFMAN

In designing this installation, Naama Hofman
was guided by three questions: What is the light
source? What form will contain it? What material
will hold them together? She treats light as an
extra dimension added to space, and compresses
it into glowing lines for minimalist 'lighting
tools'. For 004 (above) and 001 (above right),
seemingly simple designs that allow for a variety
of positions and spatial arrangements, an acrylic
tube was used to hide the source, while focusing
on the light itself. For 006 (right), an LED strip
was shielded with layers of glass and Perspex.

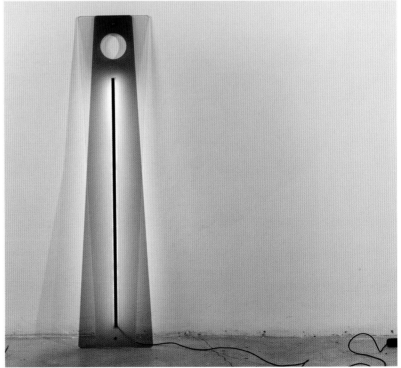

TRANSMISSION
STUDIO DEFORM

For these lamp designs, Václav Mlynár and Jakub Pollág of Studio deFORM, together with manufacturers Kavalierglass and Lasvit, combined form, transparency and glass-processing expertise to produce powerful lumino-kinetic effects. Prefabricated laboratory flasks in highly resistant borosilicate glass were cut and welded into complex unified shapes in a celebration of the material's exceptional light-transmitting properties.

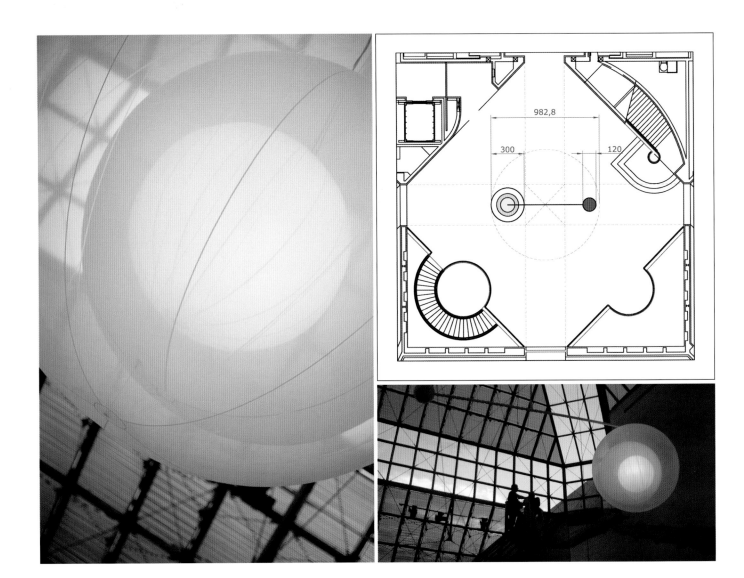

MOBILE LAMP

LUXEMBOURG CITY, LUXEMBOURG
NATHALIE DEWEZ

The subtle juxtaposition of the material and immaterial is central to the work of lighting designer Nathalie Dewez. Mobile Lamp was created for the Great Hall of the Museum d'Art Moderne Grand-Duc Jean (MUDAM). This exhibition space required a monumental chandelier that could be raised to make room for extra-large artworks, or lowered for more intimate settings. The glass ceiling imposed severe weight limitations. Challenged to create a design that would almost 'disappear when necessary', Dewez teamed up with Airstar, inventors of lighting balloons, to produce an inflatable luminaire balanced at the tip of a 10 m (33 ft)-long rod. It is made of three nested spheres, the largest measuring 3 m (10 ft) in diameter. Each 'balloon' uses a specific translucent fabric, adapting the chandelier's light intensity throughout the day. The rod can be removed to hang the triple sphere in the centre of the Hall.

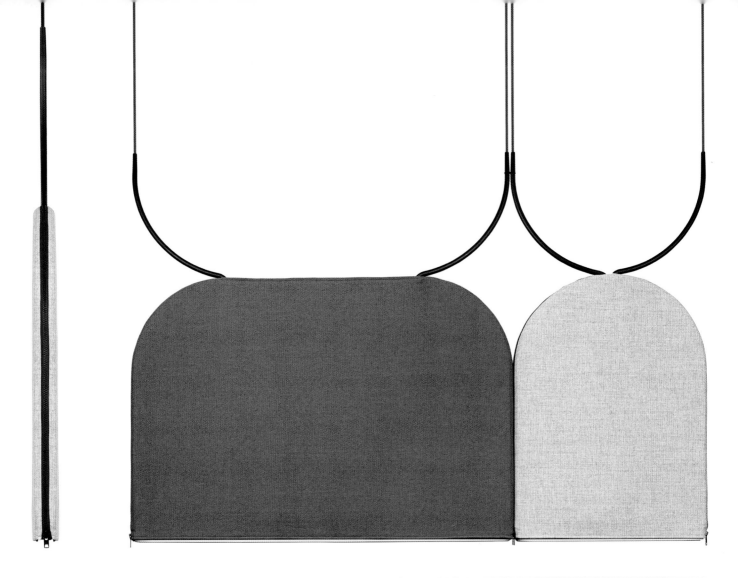

BLOCK

JOHANNA JACOBSON BACKMAN

The LED-powered Block merges lighting
seamlessly with acoustic protection. Made from
recycled SoundFelt material, which absorbs both
high and low frequencies, the design is available
in two different lengths (60 or 120 cm; 24 or 47
in.) and heights (40 or 80 cm; 16 or 31 in.). Playful
cabling encourages the hanging of the light
fixtures in groups, rather than one at a time.

HOOD
FORM US WITH LOVE

This design by Swedish collective Form Us With Love brings the notion of intimacy into open-plan offices, which, although flexible, are lacking in emotional comfort. Hood is a giant sound-absorbing lampshade in moulded polyester felt panels, which carve 'an illuminated island within any open space'. The expandable modular structure upgrades the design from a one-off piece to a commercial product.

D&D (DONNA & DONALD)

BEN WIRTH

German designer Ben Wirth enables various
lighting moods with this kinetic pendant fixture.
Two elements with mutually adjustable heights –
a black vertically suspended light rod and a white
horizontally floating glass plate – balance each
other out. The LED-powered aluminium rod plays
the double role of heat sink and counterweight.
When placed below the rod, the plate reflects
and disperses the light; as soon as it reaches the
same level as the illuminant or higher, the fixture
transforms into a directed spotlight.

ASCENT

DANIEL RYBAKKEN

A single, fluid gesture is enough to manage this lamp design by Norwegian designer Daniel Rybakken. By moving the head along the stem, the user can control both the output and the spread of light. When the head is at the bottom position, the light is turned off. As it slides upwards, light intensity increases, reaching its maximum at the top.

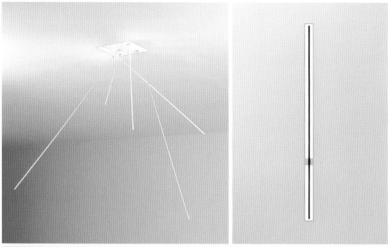

FLASH
DAVIDE GROPPI

The thunderbolt-like Flash (below) by Italian designer Davide Groppi is a striking solution to the problem of a ceiling conduit never being in the right place. The articulated body of this LED-powered luminaire delivers light to precisely where it is needed.

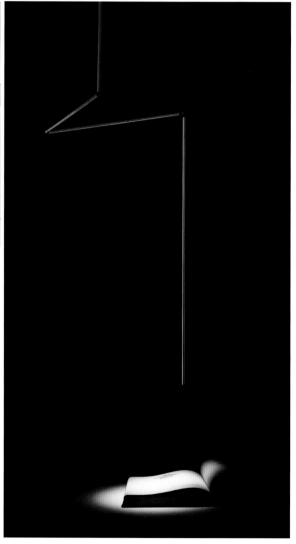

SPILLO
MARCO PAGNONCELLI

The evolution of LED technology, with its ever-smaller light sources, enables new and previously unthinkable shapes and design solutions. Developed by Marco Pagnoncelli for Icone, Spillo (above) is a series of wall and ceiling fixtures that owe their fineness to high-luminous-efficiency LED micro-strips fixed onto adjustable brass rods, 7 mm (¼ in.) in diameter.

IPNOS
ROSSI BIANCHI LIGHTING DESIGN

Ipnos (below), created by Nicoletta Rossi and
Guido Bianchi for Italian brand Flos, is another
example of a nearly dematerialized light fixture.
Its skeletal shape strips the traditional lantern
of every element that was no longer necessary.
'We ended up with a simple metal box supporting
invisible light sources, a void filled by the
surrounding space,' say the designers.

NULLA
DAVIDE GROPPI

Davide Groppi represents an ultra-minimalist
school of thought that focuses entirely on the
effects of light in space, reducing the luminaire
itself to its minimum. Occasionally, as in the case
of Nulla (above), meaning 'nothing' in Italian, the
'container' may disappear completely. A hole
in the ceiling, 18 mm (¾ in.) in diameter, is the
fixture's only visible part. The design brought
Groppi a prestigious Compasso d'Oro award 'for
designing the light and not the lamp'.

INTERNATIONAL TRIENNALE
OF KOGEI PRE-EVENT

KANAZAWA, JAPAN
NENDO

The Japanese term *kogei* describes the applied art in which craftsmen celebrate the beauty of organic natural materials. Oki Sato and his Tokyo-based collective Nendo were invited to design an exhibition for the inaugural event of the International Trienniale of Kogei, held in Kanazawa. Sixty-two craft objects in a large variety of materials, sizes and techniques were presented at the 21st Century Museum of Contemporary Art. To accommodate this extreme diversity, while also allowing each piece to stand out, Sato chose to place the objects in sixty-two standard collapsible, mass-produced mini-greenhouses. Set at equal distances apart, the uniform glass boxes created a flat perspective for viewing the exhibition. Each showcase contained one item, lit by an individual spotlight. The footprint of each box was marked by a luminous rectangle, a poetic bonus that enhanced the overall sense of order, as well as the preciousness of each object on display.

SHADE
PAUL COCKSEDGE

This lamp design (below) by Paul Cocksedge for Italian brand Flos began as 'a purely practical problem: how to rid ourselves of the clutter usually connected to light fittings.' The solution utilizes both floor and ceiling, but appears to be connected to neither. The secret is an LED floor fitting housed in a small, black cylinder. Shining upwards, it illuminates the washi paper shade that is suspended on ultra-thin nylon wires.

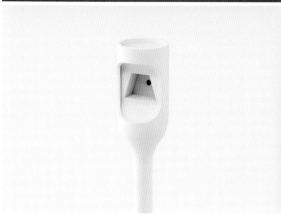

LIGHT
YOY

Tokyo-based Yoy create products that are shaped by curiosity and a sense of humour. One design is a light that appears to shine from behind peeling wallpaper; another is a 'flying' lamp with its motor hidden beneath the lampshade. This bare pole with a concealed LED (above) creates the appearance of a conventional lamp by projecting the silhouette of a lampshade onto the wall.

MARBLE WITH FLUORESCENT TUBE
BRIAN RICHER

Brian Richer of Castor Design locates his project between engineering and fine art (below). Sitting on a marble base, a fluorescent bulb emits light while its pins remain unconnected. 'The effect is achieved through the wireless transmission of electricity, a field pioneered by Nikola Tesla,' he explains. A magnetic field transfers an electrical current from the circuit, housed in the base, to the tube, which continues to glow when lifted several inches away.

TRANSPARENT LAMP
NENDO

A privacy protection film, more normally used to prevent unwelcome peeks into our windows and at our smartphones, creates fascinating visual effects in the Transparent Lamp by Nendo (above). The film turns semi-transparent when looked at directly, and transparent when viewed from an angle. Light from a centrally positioned source hits the film at a right angle, forming a contrast between the lamp's blurred glowing centre and its transparent periphery.

ANYTIME

ALEX SCHULZ

For this project (right), Swiss designer Alex Schulz crossbred a wardrobe with a floor lamp to create a multifunctional spatial solution, while reducing the use of materials. The result is a lightweight clothing rack, which incorporates LEDs and is protected by a foldable perforated envelope that doubles up as a giant lampshade.

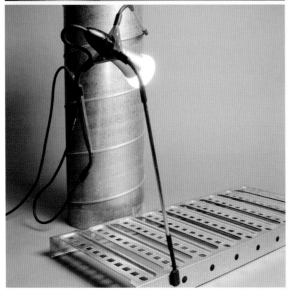

SPYDER

DAAST

Andrew Southwood-Jones and Alexander Kashin of Daast developed Spyder (left) for their own studio, which needed a mobile, easy-to-manage lighting system. A light bulb is fitted with flexible magnetic legs so it can be attached to various surfaces in different positions, and the parts connected with rubberized sheaths to create flexible joints and house magnets.

YOGA CENTRE

BEIRUT, LEBANON
.PSLAB, CBA GROUP

Specialists in bespoke lighting solutions from .PSLAB studio collaborated with architectural firm CBA Group to define the different functional areas in a yoga centre in Beirut. For a library that occupies a small and narrow space, the team proposed a wall-mounted design, in which lighting fixtures with exposed bulbs were combined with storage elements. The fixtures are aligned on two levels, so that the lower shelves would serve as counters for seated users of the centre. A few long-stem fixtures were added to the overall scheme to ensure sufficient light for reading. The double-curved design echoes the vaulted ceiling of the library, and the warm light and neat, rounded geometry help create a quiet, relaxed ambience.

STEREO KITCHEN

BEIRUT, LEBANON
.PSLAB, PAUL KALOUSTIAN

Lighting engineers .PSLAB teamed up with architect Paul Kaloustian for the design of this venue, which hosts fine dining on weekdays and clubbing at the weekends. Located on top of an office building in Beirut, the space consists of a circular, open-plan glass pavilion surrounded by a 360° panoramic terrace. To maintain the unobstructed views, lighting, climate control and sound systems were incorporated into the ceiling, which became the key element in switching between 'restaurant' and 'nightclub' modes. This was achieved through demountable V-shaped modules in perforated steel, which cover the ceiling and house the equipment. Recessed lighting fixtures were distributed in the ceiling according to the varying functions of the venue. The triangular sections of the modules and the light filtering through the reflective perforated surfaces enrich and visually lighten the concrete slab of the ceiling.

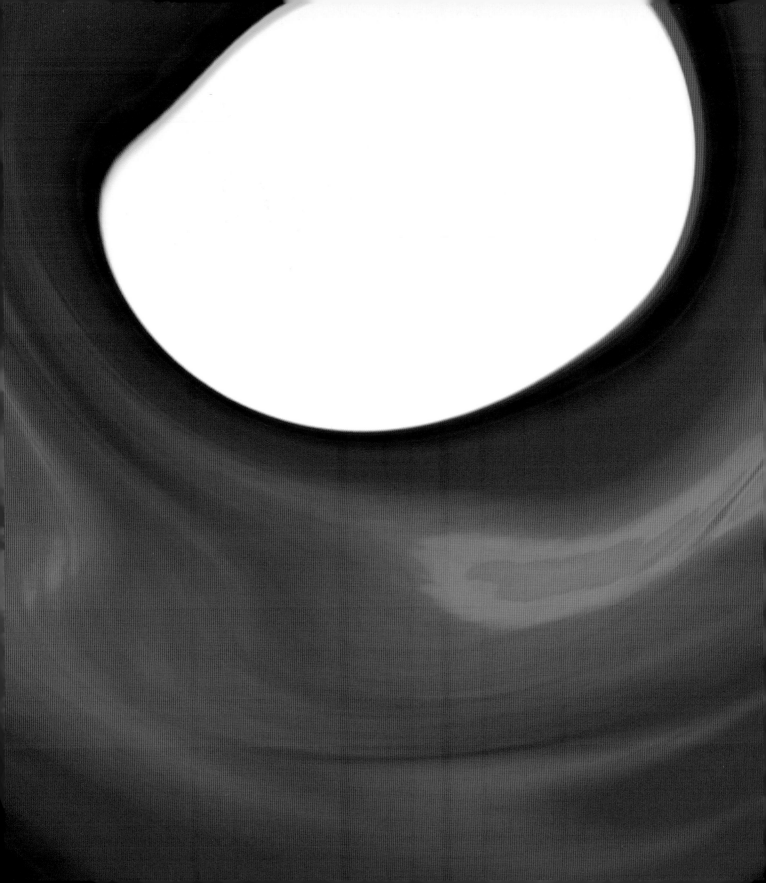

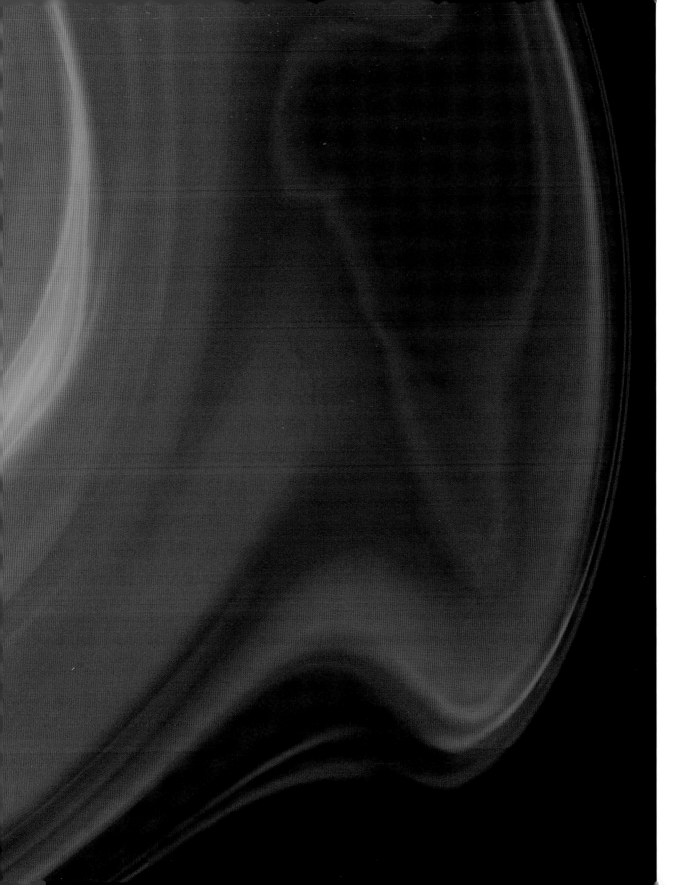

FRACTURE
WILL ROOT

The Fracture light by designer Will Root (left) creates a direct link between the act of adjusting brightness and the form of a luminaire. With the pull of a cord, a compact polyhedral mechanism unfolds and expands to crack open the dark, spherical shell and release the light.

ELAINE
DANIEL BECKER

This ball-shaped pendant lamp by Daniel Becker (right), made from 150 tea lights with built-in miniature bulbs, was originally created for a university course assignment. Inspired by the design of early artificial satellites, the project was later upgraded in cooperation with Dutch manufacturer Quasar. As student work evolved into commercial product, the tea lights were replaced by faceted metal reflectors on a lightweight frame, whose stainless-steel profiles double as electricity conductors.

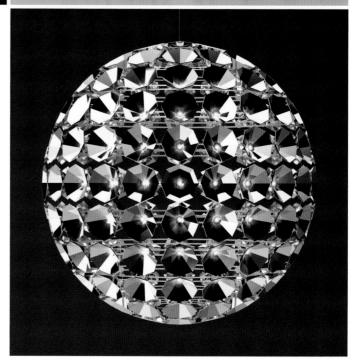

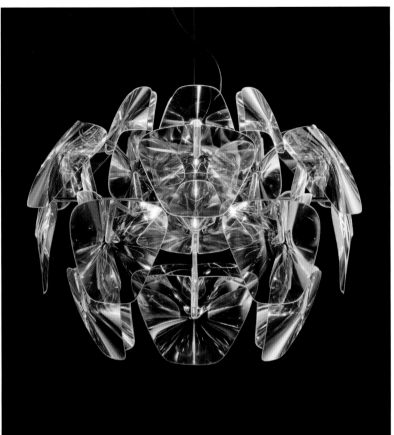

HOPE

FRANCISCO GOMEZ PAZ, PAOLO RIZZATTO

In the Hope series, developed by Francisco Gomez Paz and Paolo Rizzatto for Italian lighting brand Luceplan, nature, technology and aesthetics are combined to form a unified whole. The innovative solution offers a contemporary alternative to traditional chandeliers, which use crystal and hand-blown glass to fragment the light source into hundreds of smaller light points. Here, the designers replaced heavy and fragile crystals with ultra-light polycarbonate sheets. Based on the Fresnel lens principle, they engineered polycarbonate 'leaves', which are capable of reproducing the optical qualities of solid glass. Natural diatomic structures dictated the most efficient way of assembling these leaves around the light source to avoid glare and ensure a good diffusion of light.

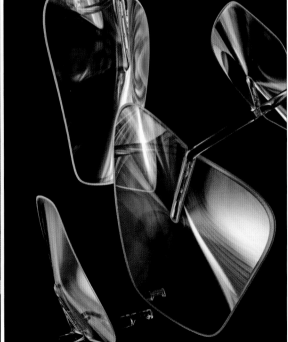

FRAGMENT

DUBAI, UAE
UNITED VISUAL ARTISTS

This suspended, 8 m (25 ft)-high structure was commissioned for an atrium in a Dubai shopping mall. Continuing its research into scientific models of nature and the use of light as a tangible and controllable material, London-based collective United Visual Artists aimed to create complexity from the repetition of simple geometries. The team assembled 421 octahedron modules into an inverted pyramid. During the day, the feature catches natural light and reflects it into the space; at night, it comes alive with white LED light, animated to create optical illusions and encourage viewers to move around as they attempt to construct a whole from their fragmented impressions.

ADVENTURE

DARLINGHURST, AUSTRALIA
KORBAN FLAUBERT

In this gallery-filling installation for the Australian Design Centre by Janos Korban and Stefanie Flaubert, tubular steel meets tubular light to create a complex three-dimensional web. The project is, in fact, an exploded version of Weblight, a flippable, zigzag-shaped, LED-powered lighting module, also designed by the duo and inspired by linear growth patterns in nature. Thirteen such modules form a dense and dynamic fabric to emulate natural phenomena, where 'one simple module and one basic rule can generate fascinating levels of complexity', and orderly patterns can emerge through the seemingly chaotic process of self-organization.

STARBRICK

OLAFUR ELIASSON

Intended both as an individual object and as a 'building material' for a range of interior-design elements, including chandeliers and partition screens, Starbrick is the product of Olafur Eliasson's research into 'the relationships between space, light modulation and geometry'. In collaboration with lighting specialists Zumtobel, Eliasson explored the different qualities of LED light, while also developing complex brick geometries at his studio in Berlin. The results of these experiments were star-shaped modules with integrated LEDs. When stacked, they form three-dimensional, kaleidoscopic structures, in which clusters of white light are counterbalanced by opaque sections in black polycarbonate; negative spaces reveal glimpses of the luminous yellow core. Offering both functional and ambient light, expandable in any direction, the system adapts to all sorts of contexts, from a home office to a concert hall.

SNEAKEROLOGY

SYDNEY, AUSTRALIA
FACET STUDIO

'When repeated 281 times over, something that
has little meaning on its own creates a euphoric
effect,' say the architects from Facet Studio
about their design for the Sneakerology store in
Sydney. Trainers are neatly presented in identical
boxes, displayed as if they are exhibits in a
museum. Individual boxes are stacked to form
a display wall, which can be straight or curved,
transparent or solid at the back. Lightboxes
with numbers assigned to each pair of shoes
provide the unifying element of the installation.
Touchscreen terminals allow the exploration of
detailed information for each 'number'.

SPACE FRAME
WHITEVOID

Berlin-based studio WHITEvoid bridges art and technology to create dynamic spatial experiences that involve the synchronized animation of large arrays of light. Under the creative direction of Christopher Bauder, interior architects join forces with media, product and lighting designers to create three-dimensional luminous structures enabled by the company's Kinetic Light modules. For CeBIT Expo 2014, WHITEvoid designed Space Frame, a multi-storey exhibition stand for Vodafone. The project featured a floor-to-ceiling light sculpture – 'inconspicuous but omnipresent' – whose glowing armature incorporated a staircase.

COLOR MANIFESTO

PARIS, FRANCE
WHITEVOID

Another design by WHITEvoid, Color Manifesto
was developed for the car manufacturer
Renault. The brand's flagship showroom in Paris
exhibited six concept vehicles, each marketed
in connection with a particular stage of our life
cycle, from falling in love to gaining wisdom. To
evoke the highly emotional character of a human
life path, the design team crafted a sculptural,
wave-like ceiling comprised of 740 RGB LED rods.
This feature displays slow chromatic animation,
informed by the principles of colour psychology.

WALL PIERCING
RON GILAD

When the design collective Under-Cover
developed a lightweight and reliable composite
material for integrating architectural elements
seamlessly with plasterboard ceilings and walls,
it did not take long for the technical knowledge to
be acquired by Italian lighting manufacturer Flos.
Today it forms the basis of the company's Soft
Architecture range of products, including this
design by Ron Gilad. Based on an LED-stuffed
ring module that does indeed seem to pierce the
wall, Wall Piercing can expand from a compact
fixture into a room-sized installation.

MONO-LIGHTS

OS&OOS

The Mono-Lights system by Dutch design studio
OS&OOS responds to 'an ever-increasing demand
for products that are lighter, faster, smaller
and more intuitive'. The designers used silicone
foam tubing as extensions for LED-TL lamps,
and connected several lamps to form flexible,
luminous chains. Defined by a 'clear monolithic
aesthetic', Mono-Lights can be bent or contorted
to fit into any spatial situation.

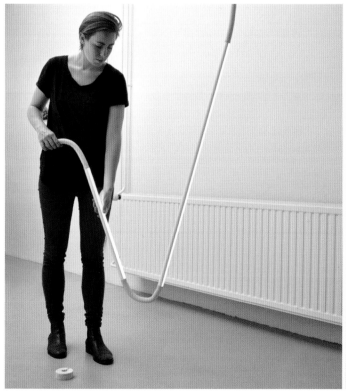

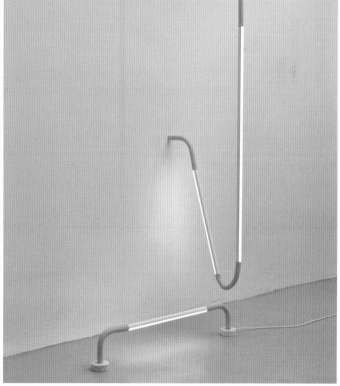

GABRIEL CHANDELIER
VERSAILLES, FRANCE
RONAN AND ERWAN BOUROULLEC

Measuring 12 m (40 ft) and weighing half a ton, this chandelier is the first contemporary work to be permanently installed at Versailles. Located at the main entrance to the palace, it is composed of 800 interlocking crystal 'beads', each fitted with an LED module that automatically adjusts to the level of daylight. In designing the chandelier, the Bouroullec brothers collaborated with crystal experts from Swarovski, as well as with the laws of gravity, which determined the final shape.

LIVING SCULPTURE

WHITEVOID

This design by Christopher Bauder of WHITEvoid
is a modular system based on Philips' super-
thin Lumiblade OLED panels and provides
a prefabricated solution for building three-
dimensional light installations. OLEDs use
electroluminescent organic film to create
uniform surfaces of bright yet non-dazzling light.
The design treats OLEDs as luminous tiles, which,
when plugged onto the rods of different lengths,
form sculptural arrangements of animated light.

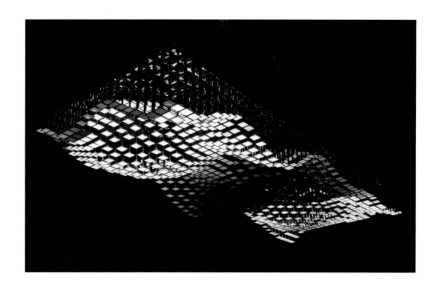

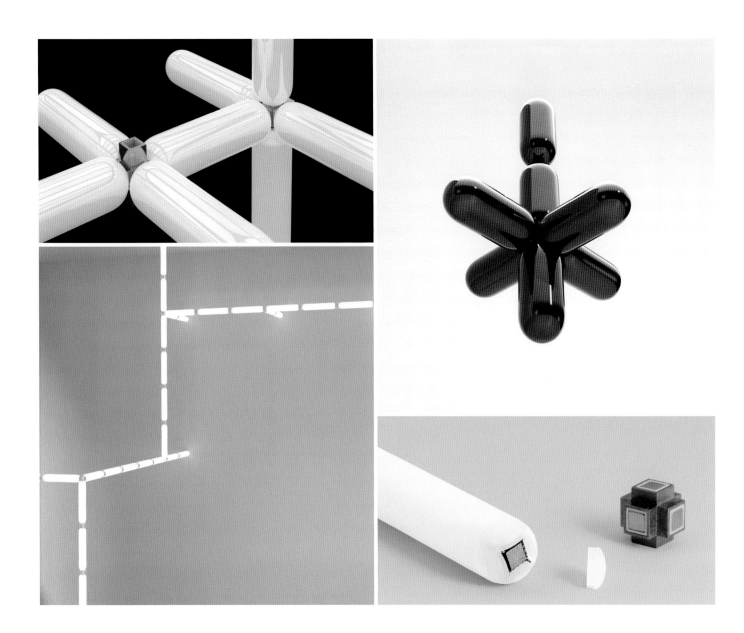

BIT LIGHT

CHOI + SHINE ARCHITECTS

This lighting system developed by US-based Choi + Shine Architects consists of self-supporting modules, or BITs, which can be added or removed with minimum effort to increase or decrease brightness. This is made possible by a set of pill-shaped polycarbonate bulbs fitted with LEDs and fastened with magnetic connectors, which both hold the modules together and transfer electric power through the system. The operating principle is the reason behind its formal diversity, as it allows the configuration of the modules into various three-dimensional forms; countless combinations are available with just a few BITs. Modules of other shapes and colours, as well as connectors that enable different assembly angles, are under development.

*TRACK WALL

BEN WIRTH

Developed by designer Ben Wirth and electrical engineer Kilian Hüttenhofer, *Track Wall combines two qualities that Wirth considers fundamental for a lighting device, being both eye-catching and feeling as if it has been custom-designed for any given space. Both qualities result from the project's functional logic: the exposed backlit circuit board not only distributes power, but is also responsible for the product's structural integrity and design identity. Light modules are freely plugged in across the power grid (or suspended to form a multi level ceiling-mounted version) and create the second, irregular and 'aerial' layer. Here, too, form reveals function, as these tiny LED-powered globes are in fact a combination of a lens and a heat sink.

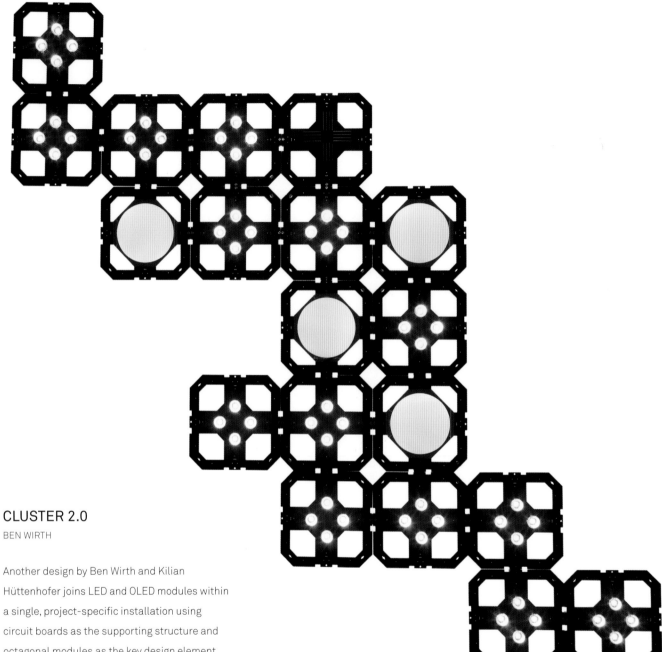

CLUSTER 2.0

BEN WIRTH

Another design by Ben Wirth and Kilian Hüttenhofer joins LED and OLED modules within a single, project-specific installation using circuit boards as the supporting structure and octagonal modules as the key design element. The visually lightweight fixture combines the directional light of LEDs with the soft, diffused light of OLEDs, and comes complete with a list of additional options, including backlight modules and rotating Cluster Turnover spotlights.

HYDRA

CARLOTTA DE BEVILACQUA

Carlotta de Bevilacqua treats light as if it were liquid. A concept shown at Euroluce 2015, the Hydra series sends light along flexible fibreoptic 'pipelines', connecting the illuminant with a light-emitting terminal located a few metres away. The plumbing metaphor is equally apt in terms of the design's capacity to 'convey light with minimum leakage', as optical fibre channels light almost without lateral loss. Halfway between an artwork and a functional object, Hydra both illuminates a space and highlights its 'ley lines'.

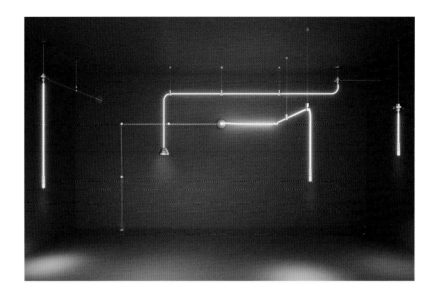

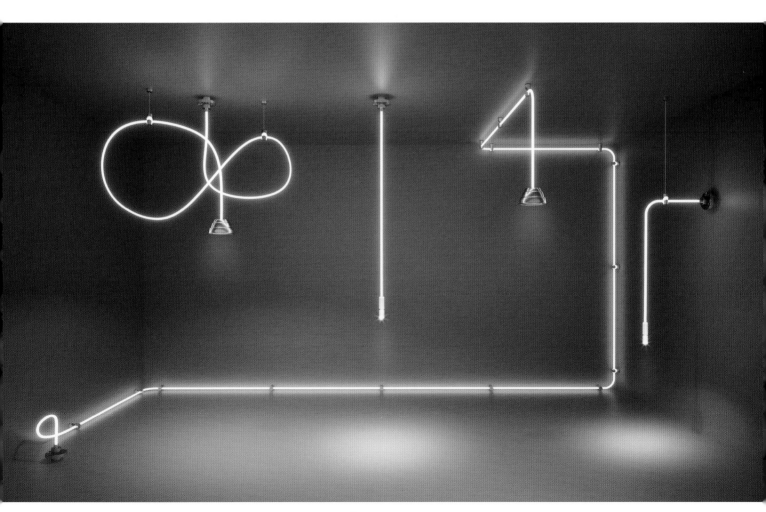

SCULPTING SPACE

XL(AMP), XXXL(AMP)

BART LENS

Conceived by architect Bart Lens, the XL (left) and XXXL (above) lamp designs are both space-defining objects. XL was initially designed to mark the edge of a trade-fair stand and project images onto the interior surface. XXXL, 4 m (13 ft) in diameter, is essentially a flattened dome, its shape inspired by Chinese lanterns. Lens notes that it should be suspended at a height of 1.5 m (5 ft), so that the space enclosed by the lamp is entered by bowing slightly, and that hanging a half- or a quarter-XXXL in a mirrored room will create the illusion of a vast space filled with giant lanterns.

CAPTURE

PAUL COCKSEDGE

The challenge behind this design by London-based Paul Cocksedge was to make the lamp infrastructure disappear completely, leaving viewers to wonder at the optical consequences. The fixture is powered by LED points concealed within the rim of the tilted aluminium dome. When peering inside the hemisphere, 1.6 m (5 ft 3 in.) in diameter, nothing is visible apart from a white diffused glow. Appearing to be contained within the lamp, the glow eliminates any sense of depth to create a stunning contrast between the lamp's three-dimensional exterior and its deceptively flat interior.

24 LINES
MONTPELLIER, FRANCE
1024 ARCHITECTURE

Oxidized steel pipes held together by plumbing collars, wooden planks and neon tubes were the building materials chosen by 1024 Architecture for the design of a work of functional art for the entrance hall and cafeteria of La Panacée, a new cultural centre in Montpellier, France. The result is a hybrid of a garden pavilion and covered passage that fences off a more intimate 'space within a space' in the venue's busy lobby, while remaining transparent and fully integrated within the overall context. The 40 m (131 ft)-long structure is punctuated with twenty-four flexible neon tubes that outline its shape and create a sense of rhythm, especially noticeable when the fixture displays animated sequences of light that vibrate in unison with current events.

STRING

MICHAEL ANASTASSIADES

'Every time I take the train, I sit by the window and watch the series of perfectly parallel strings connecting the pylons,' says Michael Anastassiades. 'I love the way they divide the landscape and how spheres are occasionally beaded through the wires at random intervals.' This is just one of the designer's sources of inspiration in connection with this series for Flos. LED-powered pendant spheres and cones come with seemingly endless electric cords, stretched between walls and ceilings to articulate the room through a kind of spatial drawing. On a more pragmatic level, String is an ingenious solution for bringing overhead light to rooms that are not equipped with a pendant fitting.

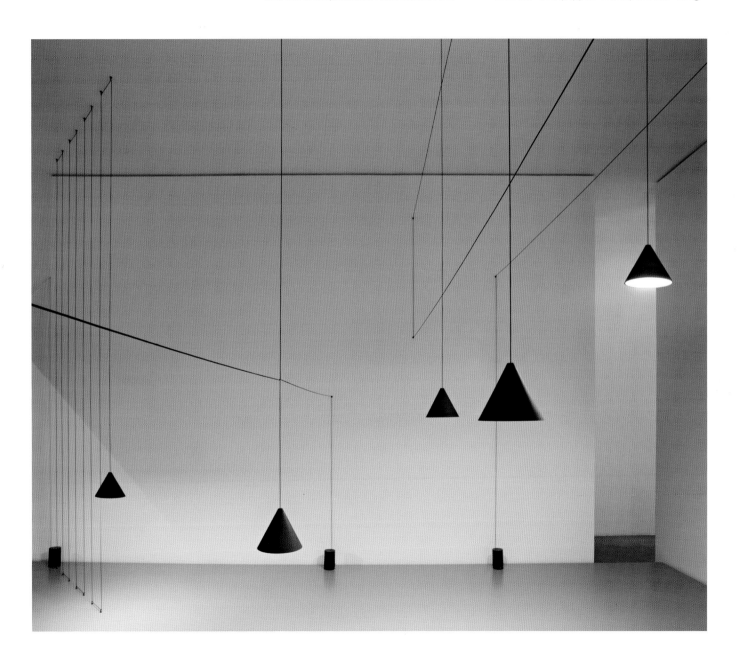

UNDERGROUND SPA

LIMERICK, IRELAND
CARMODY GROARKE

Carved from beneath a nineteenth-century house, the design concept of this private underground spa relies on a fine-tuned combination of stone and lighting, with daylight punching through from the ground-level courtyard to flood the rooms. In the main space, the black textured lining of the swimming pool creates a strong contrast with the smooth white surfaces of the limestone walls. A halo of indirect light models the geometrically 'folded' plaster ceiling that appears to float above the water.

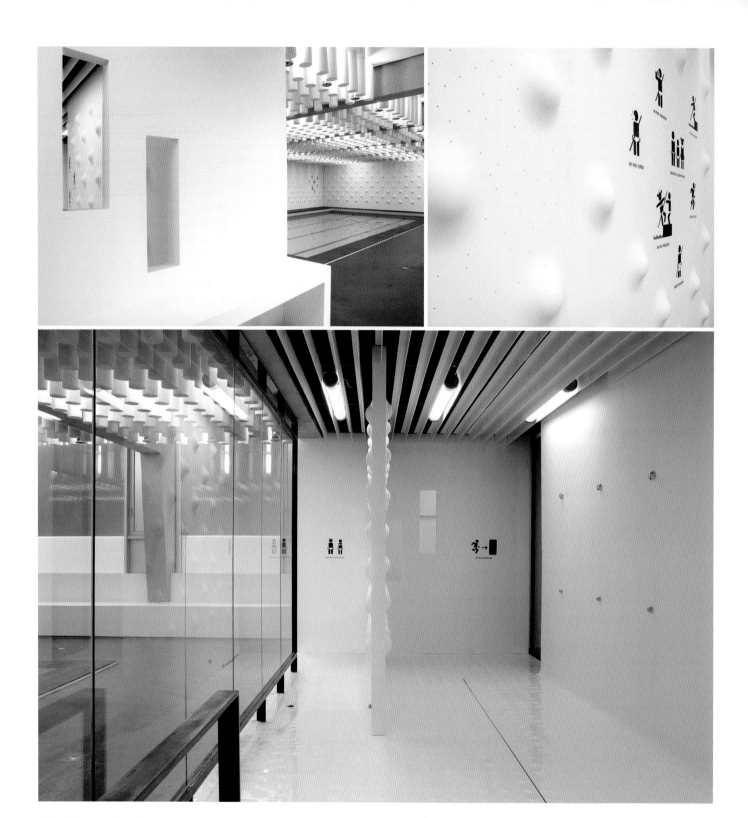

ATLAS SPORTS CENTRE

PARIS, FRANCE
YOONSEUX ARCHITECTES

For the design upgrade of a sports centre in Paris, the client asked French architectural firm Yoonseux to improve the functionality of the swimming pool as part of an extensive renovation project. The facility had neither extra space nor exterior views to work with, so the architects focused on creating a compact and user-friendly sequence of functional zones, as well as rethinking the tactile appeal of each surface. The fluid, strategically organized layout, in which partitions are minimized or made from transparent materials, facilitates the distribution of light across the entire space. White acrylic resin, a malleable and robust material, responded to a range of practical issues and allowed for a truly sculptural approach in shaping the surfaces. To improve the acoustics in the swimming-pool area, the ceiling was fitted with a forest of 'acoustic pins'. Lighting fixtures are placed above the pins, which filter the light and eliminate glare. In return, light makes the most of the white and heavily textured ceiling and walls.

EMG STONE GALLERY

GUANGZHOU, CHINA
O-OFFICE ARCHITECTS

For a stone-trading firm based in Guangzhou, China, O-Office Architects transformed a former food factory into a gallery devoted to stone art. The site is located in the old industrial zone – abandoned owing to the encroaching urban sprawl and the relocation of production facilities – which is currently being converted into a cultural district. Recognizing the 1960s building, originally assembled from precast concrete parts, as part of China's 'collective industrial memory', the team maintained the existing structure and added a suspended deck that rests on a steel framework and houses the company offices. The bottom of the deck is clad in translucent polycarbonate panels, which create a luminous, LED-powered ceiling above the public spaces of the ground floor, including the art gallery and café. The silent dialogue between the solidity of the weathered concrete and the weightlessness of the light installation forms a backdrop to the works of art and 'the billion years of geological memory' they evoke.

DRAWING FASHION

LONDON, UK
CARMODY GROARKE, A PRACTICE FOR EVERYDAY LIFE

London architecture studio Carmody Groarke collaborated with design agency A Practice For Everyday Life to create a 'subtle backdrop' for the works of the most important fashion illustrators from the 1920s to the present day. The team transformed the exhibition hall in the Design Museum, London, with a series of interlinking curved 'lantern walls'. This allowed for the carving out of more intimate niches dedicated to individual artists, which were particularly suitable for displaying the illustrations. Illuminants were placed inside the 'lanterns' to provide soft ambient light and subtly trace the silhouette of the supporting structure.

WALL CLOUD

TOKYO, JAPAN
SASAKI ASSOCIATES, CHIPS LLC,
LIGHTING SOU

Architect Ryuichi Sasaki revisited a former warehouse building that was once home to legendary discotheque Juliana's Tokyo to deal with a difficult space in the attic. Owing to the low ceiling height (2.1 m, or 7 ft) with only 1.7 m (5 ft 6 in.) under the beams, the space felt oppressive and remained empty for some time. Sasaki found a solution in lifting the partition walls off the ground. By removing the false ceiling, he exposed the heavy beams, which allowed them to be treated as an integral part of the new system of floating walls. Asked to divide the space between two tenants, he simply completed the lower portion of one of the suspended walls with transparent glass. Together with Kazuhiro Nagashima of CHIPS LLC and Natsuha Kameoka of Lighting Sou, Sasaki devised a lighting scheme that enhanced the 'wall-cloud' effect by incorporating light into the bottom surfaces of the floating partitions.

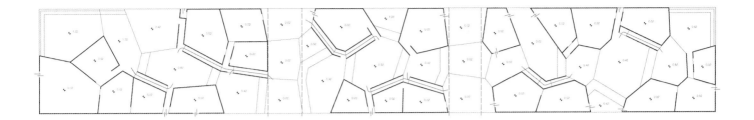

WHITE GEOLOGY

PARIS, FRANCE
PHILIPPE RAHM

The capacity of a white surface to reflect and diffuse light shaped architect Philippe Rahm's design for 'La Force de l'Art 02', the second triennial exhibition of contemporary art held in 2009, in Paris. Beneath the majestic glass vaults of the Grand Palais, in a space flooded with natural light, Rahm deployed a landscape-like platform, whose uniformly white surface had the reflective power of snow (80 per cent). The complex formation was derived from a basic rectangle measuring 125 × 24 m (410 × 79 ft), on which each artwork was initially allocated the same space and volume. Then the geological process began. 'Depending on their actual size and viewing distance, the exhibits began pushing against one another, just like shifting tectonic plates,' explains Rahm. The weight of each work, together with the required amount of light, determined to what extent it distorted the surface. Instead of fitting the artworks into the architecture, as with conventional exhibition design, Rahm let architecture 'yield to the demands of each work of art'.

DOMESTIC ASTRONOMY

HUMLEBÆK, DENMARK
PHILIPPE RAHM

This project, shown at the Louisiana Museum of Modern Art in Denmark, invited viewers to reconsider the factors that shape our homes. The premise behind it was Archimedes' principle: hot air rises, while cold air descends. In a typical flat, this can result in a significant temperature difference between floor and ceiling. Instead of wasting these calories, they could be utilized by placing each zone at a height where the temperature is best suited for a given activity. Here, temperature difference is controlled through lighting, since, like the sun, electric light generates heat.

Incandescent lamps produce dramatically more heat than light, while contemporary technologies have a much better energy balance. Architect Philippe Rahm used clusters of incandescent and compact fluorescent bulbs, mounted at two diagonal points, to illuminate and heat the space. The incandescent cluster is programmed to heat the lower level to 19°C (66°F); the fluorescent lamps are fixed closer to the ceiling and produce 16°C (61°F). Together they create a microclimate, which enabled Rahm to engage the entire available volume for a truly three-dimensional lifestyle.

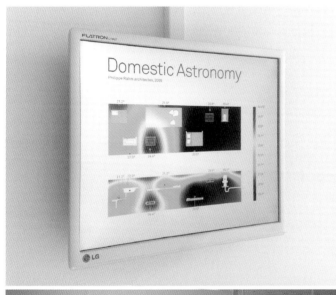

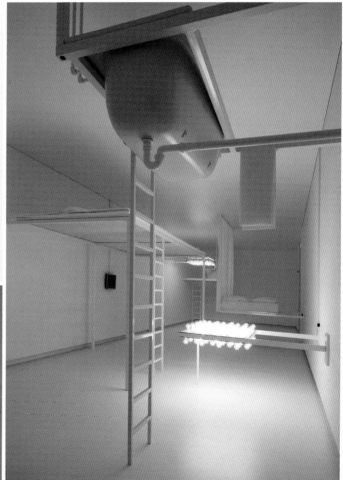

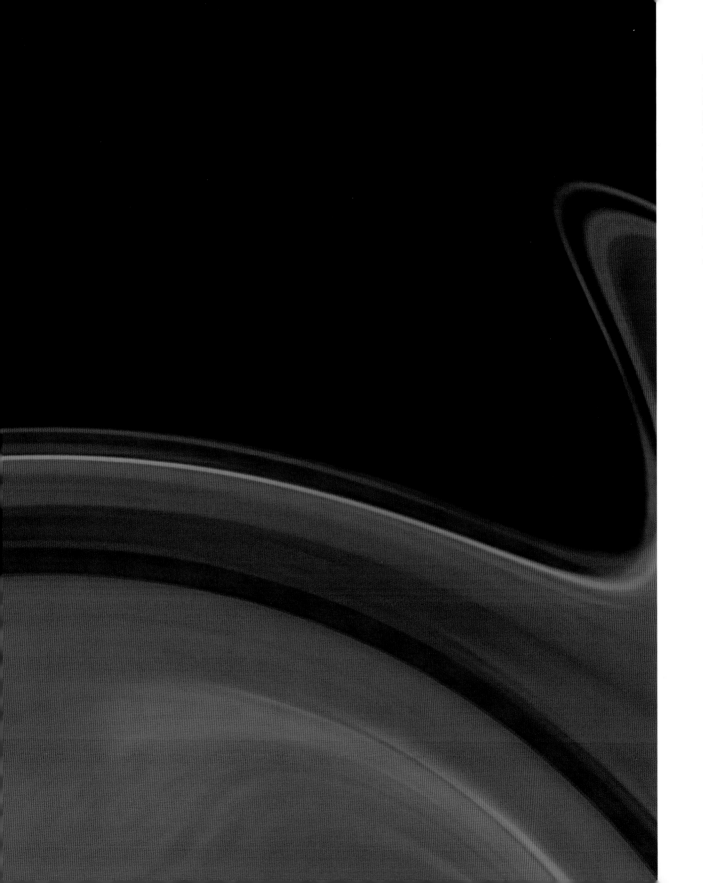

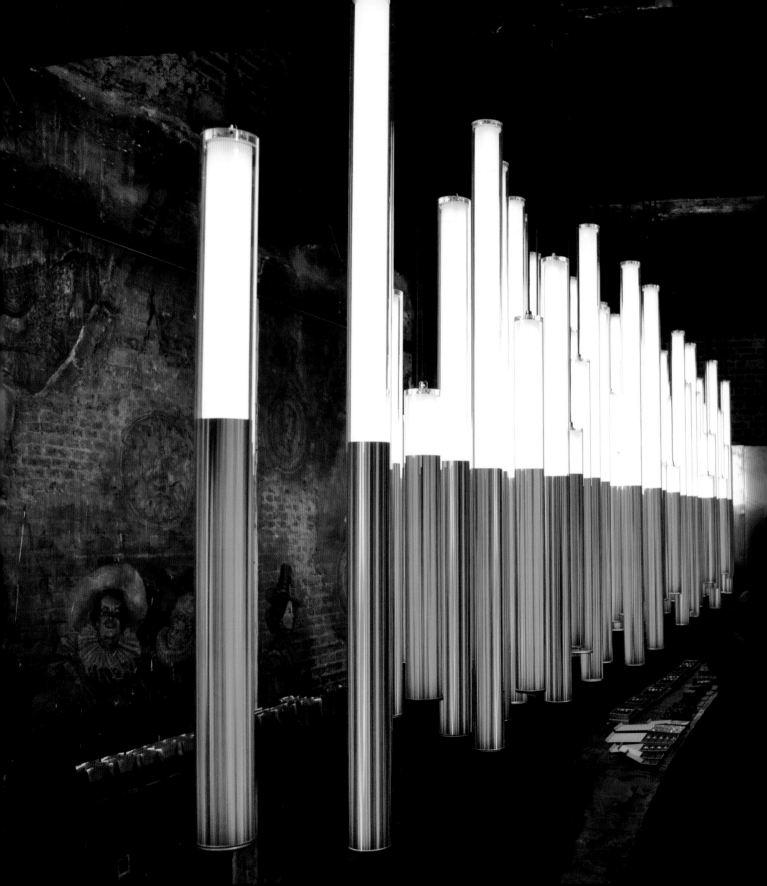

HANGING FOREST

BRUSSELS, BELGIUM
GILBERT MOITY

For his new shop in Brussels, master chocolatier
Patrick Roger chose a listed building in the
heart of the capital. Architect Gilbert Moity was
challenged to provide fluid circulation within the
shop's narrow and high ceilinged space, while
leaving the façade and interior walls untouched.
Customers are guided around the central 'island',
formed by a long, sculptural table in bronze and
an overhead fixture that highlights the central
display area, providing the primary source of
light for the entire space. The 7 × 1 m (23 × 3 ft)
installation comprises ninety light tubes, whose
irregular arrangement and colour scheme evoke
a 'hanging forest' – a reference to nature as
Roger's own source of inspiration.

SOCIAL CLUB

PARIS, FRANCE
1024 ARCHITECTURE

For a temporary fitout marking the moment
of transition from one nightclub to another,
Paris-based firm 1024 Architecture painted the
entire space black, then traced a light-sensitive
topographic grid across the walls and floor. A new
space-within-a-space came alive when 'black'
UVA light is switched on. The sources of black
light were integrated in the linear ceiling fixture,
which used a sequence of neon tubes to connect
the club's neural nodes: entrance, ticket counter,
cloakroom, bar, dance floor and DJ booth.

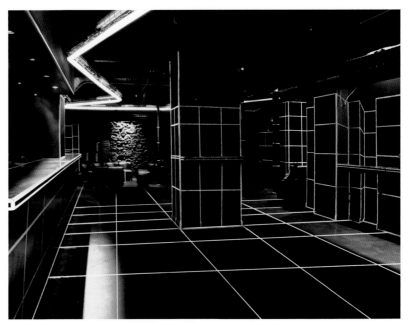

UCHI LOUNGE 01

SYDNEY, AUSTRALIA
FΛCET STUDIO

'Weightless light that floats within boundless darkness' sums up the design concept by Facet Studio for the Uchi Lounge restaurant in Sydney. The client envisaged a 'conceptual place', where diners were expected to appreciate, rather than simply consume, the food. The architects, therefore, made the spatial boundaries 'disappear' under black paint, and refocused diners' attention on the massive 8.4 × 1.6 m (28 × 5 ft) concrete table illuminated by a 13 m (43 ft)-long luminous ribbon, which hovers above their plates with no apparent support.

ZOLLVEREIN GALLERY COAL WASHER

ESSEN, GERMANY
OMA, HEINRICH BÖLL, LICHT KUNST LICHT

Once Europe's largest mining complex, the defunct Zollverein colliery is now a UNESCO World Heritage site. Some of the facilities, including Pit XII, designed in the late 1920s, are considered milestones in the history of industrial architecture. Today the Coal Washer, originally the first stage in processing the excavated coal, houses the visitors' centre, exhibition and event spaces, and serves as the gateway to a 'route of industrial culture'. OMA and architect Heinrich Böll were responsible for the architectural revamp of the colliery, while Licht Kunst Licht developed the lighting concept. One of the most striking features is the enclosed, 93 m (305 ft)-long escalator, where fiery fluorescent backlighting creates an immersive, colour-saturated transition space that contrasts with the functional light of the interiors. A similar treatment has been applied to the main stairwell, where an LED-powered fiery glow is concentrated within the stairs, while the dark walls allow for screening video projections.

ST BOTOLPH BUILDING

LONDON, UK
GRIMSHAW ARCHITECTS, SPEIRS + MAJOR

Designed by Grimshaw Architects with lighting experts Speirs + Major, the St Botolph Building is one of the largest office developments in the City of London. The interiors and the lighting concept were both intended to optimize the circulation of office workers and visitors, or, as Speirs + Major's associate director Andrew Howis says, 'improve the worker's journey' around the building.

For the vast reception area, the solution was to 'clad' the vertical surfaces in light, which created a strong visual impact, as well as helping people to make sense of the space. Making it 'impossible to tell where the light ends and the building begins', architects and lighting designers co-developed a textured cladding system with 2,500 seamlessly integrated LED lights. In the heart of the building, where corridors and bridges open onto the central atrium, the abundance of metalwork ran the risk of making the structure too imposing. To avoid this, the lighting team convinced the architects to add glazed floors with incorporated underlighting.

With the uplit atrium roof and illuminated lift cores added to the mix, the result is a light and airy ambience. The stairways have a control system that reacts to both natural light and motion: when daylight recedes, the system provides the minimum required amount of lighting, while presence detectors boost its levels to accompany a worker's movement up or down the stairs. The double advantage is the minimizing of energy consumption and animation of the façade.

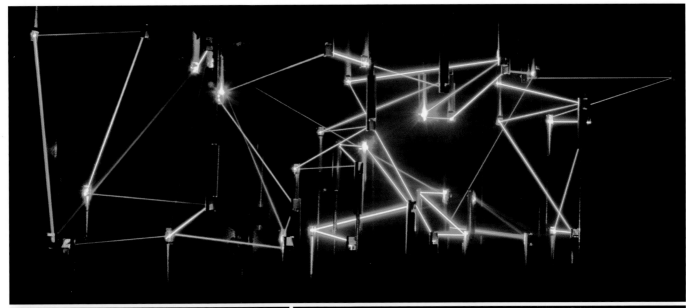

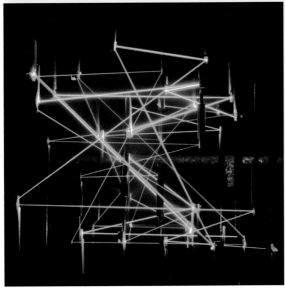

ONE BEAM OF LIGHT

LONDON, UK
GNI PROJECTS

UK-based team GNI Projects was commissioned to design a light sculpture as part of the 'One Beam of Light' exhibition at the Institute of Contemporary Art, London. It was intended as a physical representation of the essence of the exhibition, which showcased photographic images based on the creative use of light. A single beam of green laser light is sent bouncing from mirror to mirror, generating a pattern that made no sense from any position but one, in which the crisscrossed beams outlined the word 'light'. The effect was created with the help of a fine tubular structure, with ninety-eight cross joints enabling the required positioning of forty-nine bespoke mirror heads.

POSITION – N 46°38'47" E 14°53'31"
NEUHAUS, AUSTRIA
QUERKRAFT ARCHITEKTEN, BRIGITTE KOWANZ

Designed by Querkraft Architekten, the extension
for the Museum Liaunig is almost completely
buried into the hill. Gold objects from Africa, an
important part of the collection, are displayed in
a black room, accessible via a concrete corridor
that features a work by Austrian artist Brigitte
Kowanz. The museum's geographical location
is 'written' with neon tubes, which are reflected
in the mirrored ceiling to provide an additional
dimension to the underground space.

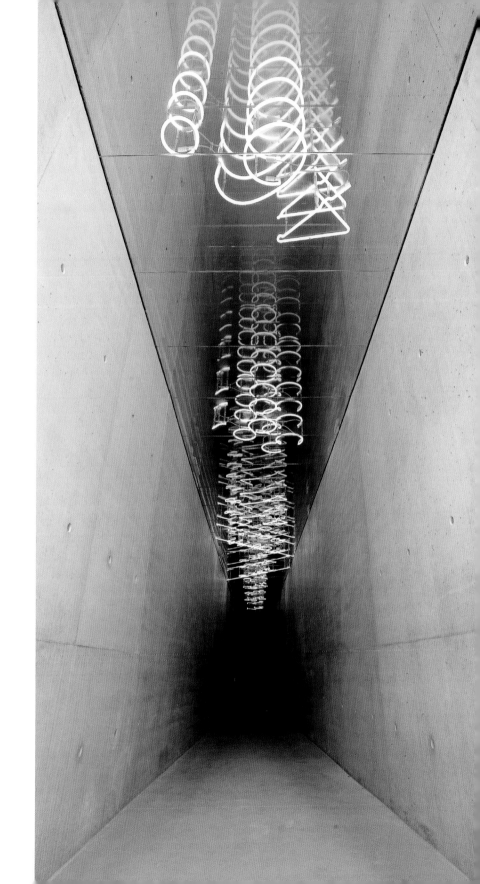

■ DANCE AND THEATRE
■ PLASTIC ARTS
■ PHOTOGRAPHY AND MEDIA LIBRARY
■ LECTURE ROOMS
■ MUSIC
■ CINEMA
■ DIGITAL ARTS

PARIS 8 UNIVERSITY ARTS DEPARTMENT

SAINT-DENIS, FRANCE
MOUSSAFIR ARCHITECTES,
BERNARD DUFOURNET

When Paris 8 University decided to transform its library building into the arts department, architects Jacques Moussafir and Bernard Dufournet produced a competition-winning solution that added a powerful sensory dimension to a standard prefabricated structure.

Loosely inserted into the existing open-plan space, classrooms and workshops are separated by irregular trapezoid gaps, some of which are filled with service functions, while others act as 'threshold zones', reconnecting the different programmes (dance, theatre, media arts) to the central corridor. Workspaces are painted white or grey, and the interstitial areas are colour-coded according to programme.

The architects relied on the fusion of colour and light to design spatial sequences defined by a new system of orientation. Translucent windows of varying size and colour provide additional visual connections, with the changing angles of view multiplying reflections. Sheathed in coloured film and placed at strategic points, compact fluorescent tubes enhance the overall feeling of 'radiant serenity'.

MATERIALIZATION

PRENZLAUER BERG RESIDENCE
BERLIN, GERMANY
WOLFF ARCHITEKTEN

Berlin's first façade built from light-transmitting concrete adorns this development by Wolff Architekten (left). The first experiments in combining concrete with light-transmitting elements were conducted in 1935, yet large-scale concrete panels with optical fibres inside them were not produced until 2013. Manufactured by Lucem, the panels have a light source (RGB LEDs with DMX-control) mounted at the rear. Travelling to the surface of the panel, light creates the spectacular effect of walls that glow from the inside.

BANK OF GEORGIA
TBILISI, GEORGIA
DEPHANI

Architectural firm Dephani used illuminated translucent concrete to renovate the Tbilisi headquarters of the Bank of Georgia (opposite), built in 1975 and a landmark of Soviet-era architecture. For the interiors, Dephani sought a solution that would resonate with the original design concept of the 'room city', in which rectangular volumes are configured into an articulate formation of solids and voids. The idea of urban light shining through the building was recreated in the interior elements, including the walk-in cube in the bank tellers' office and the corridor in the asset-management department, which were made from light-transmitting concrete to suggest lightness and transparency in an otherwise solid material.

YII EXHIBITION
NENDO

Japanese design firm Nendo was asked to create the exhibition design for 'Yii', curated by Gijs Bakker for the National Taiwan Craft Research Institute and presented at Milan Design Week 2011. The organization's mission is to revitalize traditional Taiwanese crafts in today's context, so the team produced a poetic and budget-friendly setting that brought together 'contemporary society and nature' and 'industry and craft'. In the solemn hall of the Triennale Design Museum, the designers installed dozens of 10 m (33 ft)-high columns in inflated transparent vinyl. As bamboo groves are typical of Taiwan, the designers hoped to bring to the exhibition the unique sensation of standing amid their soaring stalks. Constantly changing perspectives, reflections and specks of light on transparent surfaces created a 'floating', dream-like ambience.

WALLOVER, FLYING DOTS

TOMAS EREL, CHRISTIAN BIECHER

Developed by Saint-Gobain Innovation Centre, the light-emitting Planilum is a sandwich of four glass sheets with rarefied gas sealed inside. An electric current excites the gas, which emits UV radiation that is transformed into visible light through screenprinted phosphorous patterns, while the rest of the panel remains transparent. The result is a soothing light that 'can be touched without getting burnt'. Produced by Saazs, Wallover by Tomas Erel (right and below) and Flying Dots by Christian Biecher (below right) hint at the panels' possible uses. On a larger scale, Planilum is an 'architectural product' capable of merging light fixtures with partitions.

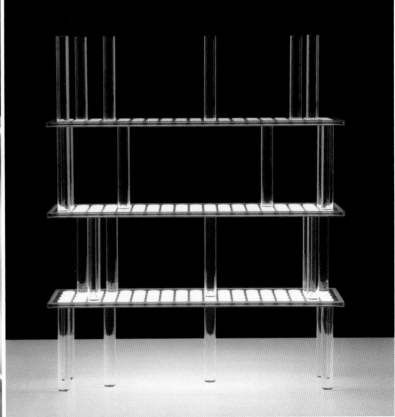

LOGAN OFFICE

NEW YORK, NEW YORK, USA
SO-IL

For a client who required more shared
workspaces than individual ones, architectural
firm SO-IL designed an office with large
desks and a seamless, full-height partition
in translucent fabric, which broke down the
scale of the interior while maintaining a shared
environment and allowing natural light to
penetrate. A luminous PVC ceiling provides
uniform light and unifies the space. 'Looking
through layers of fabric, people and objects
appear out of focus,' say the architects. 'Fabric
walls catch natural light and change colour
as light changes throughout the day. This
abstraction, combined with the symmetry of
spaces and the spatial ambiguity of the fabric,
creates a dream-like, surreal experience.'

AUDITORIUM

LONDON, UK
PAUL COCKSEDGE

When asked to design the main auditorium for the 100% Design show during the London Design Festival 2012, Paul Cocksedge responded with a concept that enabled the coexistence of 'things that on the surface seem mutually exclusive: open-shut, inside-outside, solid-transparent'. The enclosure of the Auditorium was formed by a network of tensioned nylon wires, which resembled and were inspired by a spiderweb. Light reflects off the virtually invisible material, rendering it visible while maintaining the scent of paradox: the confines of the space are clearly defined yet remain transparent, so the venue feels accessible even when the seating area is full.

LIGHT SEGMENTS SPACE

KIMCHI AND CHIPS

This project was intended to function as both an artwork and a new creative tool ('Digital Emulsion Technique'), to be made available to other artists. Mimi Son and Elliot Woods of Seoul-based studio Kimchi and Chips segmented a dark gallery interior with an architectural web of 'invisible' nylon strings, onto which were mapped a sequence of digital projections that highlight specific fragments of the filament to create dynamic spatial forms. Generating physical volumes by means of light, the installation references Picasso's 'light paintings' and the geometric abstract works of the Venezuelan artist and sculptor Gego (Gertrud Goldschmidt), particularly her *Reticulàreas* series from 1969, in which exhibition spaces were filled with an interweaving of metallic webs.

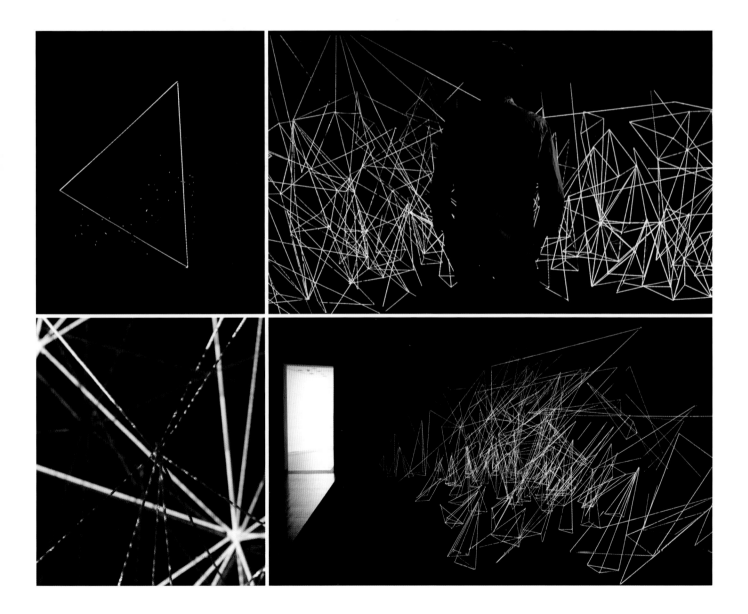

LE CIEL BLEU

OSAKA, JAPAN
NORIYUKI OTSUKA, KENJIRO IKEDA

Noriyuki Otsuka was reluctant to use a purely functional approach in this design for a fashion store in a retail complex. In a 278 m² (2,992 sq ft) space with a 5 m (16.4 ft)-high ceiling, such an approach could have resulted in an undesirable 'megastore' effect. Otsuka chose instead to base the design on other factors, such as transparency and light. The anchoring element is a centrally positioned, tunnel-like structure made from steel mesh and related to the Japanese tradition of using latticework screens to define boundaries without blocking visual connections. In a

large, open space with a limited number of freestanding objects, Otsuka added spatial accents by creating shadows. This was done through juxtaposing different colour temperatures, the lowest coming from the ceiling fixtures, the highest from neon lights, and the medium-high from the shoe display and tubular pendant in the tunnel. Light also serves as a protective barrier: Otsuka and lighting consultant Kenjiro Ikeda tripled the brightness of light around the storefront to form an 'invisible curtain' against the interfering outdoor light.

YOU AND I HORIZONTAL, BETWEEN YOU AND I, FIVE MINUTES OF PURE SCULPTURE

ANTHONY MCCALL

You and I Horizontal (above and opposite, top left); Between You and I (opposite, bottom left) and Five Minutes of Pure Sculpture (opposite right) are rooted in artist Anthony McCall's early cinematographic experiments, in which he focused on projected light and its relationships with time. Technically, McCall's installations are about projecting animated lines in a dark room filled with haze. As an experience, they are a sensory paradox: 'I call them "solid light pieces"', he says, 'because, when you first encounter these works, you see something made of veils of light that looks quite solid, almost like it's a thing.' In the 1970s, McCall's preferred media was 16 mm film; today he uses digital technologies, which allow him to deepen his investigations and to work with vertical projections, thus shifting his creative output into the realm of sculpture. Visitors enter the three-dimensional spaces formed by curved planes of light and reach out with their hands to touch the 'walls' of the luminous pyramids.

ARCADES
TROIKA

Works by the London-based trio Troika challenge our visual sensibilities. First presented at the Biennale Interieur 2012, in Kortrijk, Belgium, this project 'confronts the viewer with the seemingly impossible phenomenon of bending light', as the artists explore 'the twilight zone between what is intangible and what is physical'. Under the pitched roof of a former stable block, fourteen pillars of light are set along a dark space to create an almost palpably luminous architecture. Travelling through Fresnel lenses, the light beams change direction, while myriad light particles suspended in the humid air heighten the effect, facilitating the journey from disbelief to contemplation.

LEXUS L-FINESSE

TOKUJIN YOSHIOKA

Japanese designer Tokujin Yoshioka's installation for the Lexus exhibition at Milan Design Week 2006 gave visitors the chance to experience a tangible sensation of light. Having filled the space with 700 km (435 miles) of backlit transparent plastic fibres, Yoshioka encouraged exhibition-goers to make their way through this 'thickened light' to arrive at a sculptural model of the company's latest automobile design. The idea stemmed from the designer's interest in the design potential of fibres in general, as well as his memories of an earlier project involving multiple strands of illuminated optic fibre. Fascinated by the effect, Yoshioka began thinking about the ways to create a space 'that would be composed of three-dimensional light'. At that point, the commission from Lexus came as the perfect occasion in which to bring his dream to life.

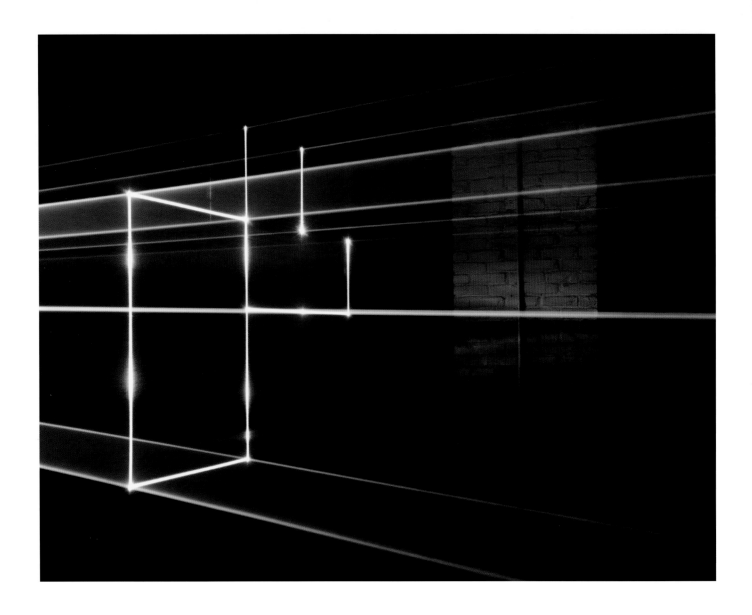

VANISHING POINT

UNITED VISUAL ARTISTS

With this project, the artists' passion for creating structures from light led the London-based team to use light as a medium for creating architectural forms. Inviting the viewer into a pitch-dark room, they used this darkness as a canvas on which programmed laser beams 'reshape, redefine and represent a space' through perspective drawings. Inspired by the drawings of Renaissance Old Masters, the project 'sends lines into space from an arbitrary vanishing point, creating different volumes, divisions and rooms to be experienced by the audience'. Tiemen Rapati of United Visual Artists says: 'What interests us is where the programmable and the real come together. It's this physicality of light that we have been exploring in many different ways. Light is ultimately controllable, and you can use it to create anything you want, but it also has a physical, very visceral attraction.'

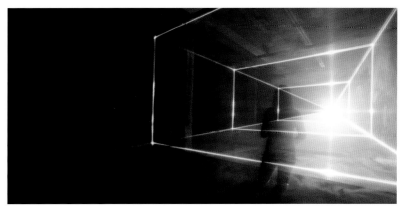

TRANSFORMING

TIME

When Olafur Eliasson switched on the artificial sun for his famous *Weather Project* (2003–4) in Tate Modern's Turbine Hall, museumgoers reacted spontaneously by basking in the electric rays that shone through the clouds of machine-produced spectral mist. The effect was so realistic and powerful that even the installation's exposed substructure and wiring did not change people's behaviour. What makes this exhibition particularly interesting is the fact that the artist used light to freeze a moment in time and create an effect of perpetual daylight for a period of several months.

Light as a medium of time is the theme of the second chapter, with 'Daylight' as our starting point. Presented here is a range of projects, in which architectural solutions are guided by the intention to maximize the impact of natural light. Much of their appeal comes from the light that changes throughout the 24-hour cycle. Some of these designs boast highly elaborate detailing, such as curved reflective roofs, or precisely calculated shapes and positions of skylights carefully coordinated with the motion of the sun to ensure the desired lighting effects. In certain cases – including a few introverted houses that prefer views of the sky to those of the uninspiring neighbourhood – the changing daylight represents the only visual connection with the outside world.

While in these projects the modulations of light visualize the flux of time, other designs, such as Daniel Rybakken's daylight-related experiments (pp. 126–7) or Paolo Di Trapani's sophisticated emulation of the sunlit sky (p. 129), imitate natural light through artificial means to achieve some particular lighting scenarios and thus create an altered, 'suspended' sense of time. The next section, 'Rhythm', is focused on the design of cyclic patterns of light or using light to articulate a certain sequence of events. The concepts can relate to some natural phenomenon, such as the water that evaporates and condenses in the lamp collection by Arturo Erbsman (p. 138), or to the dynamic urban rhythms in Gerd Pfarré's scheme for the subway station (pp. 140–1), where the colour of light changes to announce the arrival of trains. For an open-plan apartment (pp. 142–3), Nicolas Dorval-Bory and Raphaël Bétillon use different types of light sources as the key instrument to defining the day and night zones, while Éléonore Delisse designed a colour-changing lamp to aid in readapting our internal clocks to the natural circadian rhythms (p. 139).

The vector of design research that explores rhythm, as well as the moments and spaces of transition, may produce some intriguing solutions for the contemporary 'city without cycles', in which the distinctions between day and night, work and home, are becoming blurred, if not erased. Change is the best, even the only, marker of the flow of time. This section, appropriately titled 'Change', looks into some of the infinite ways of expressing change through light. Complex animated LED sequences upgrade the crossing of a dark underground passage to a sensory experience. One simple gesture is enough to switch between different lighting moods and change the appearance of the luminaire at the same time.

Natural laws and reactive surfaces are at work in projects by United Visual Artists (pp. 158–9) and Simon Heijdens (pp. 160–1) that sensitize us both to ourselves and to the outside world. Carlo Ratti envisages previously unheard of, dynamic three-dimensional displays enabled by the latest in the LED technology (p. 148) and Laurent Fort uses a hand-crafted device to bring the entire room alive with moving organic forms (p. 163), while Philippe Rahm simply switches on the lights to create night in the middle of the day (p. 152).

SHONAN CHRIST CHURCH

KANAGAWA, JAPAN
TAKESHI HOSAKA

The distinguishing feature of Shonan Christ Church is the concrete roof, formed by six curved slabs, which was conceived by Takeshi Hosaka and achieved in collaboration with Arup. The striking design provides a number of structural and acoustic benefits and enables an elaborate daylighting scheme, which was central to the architect's concept. Orchestrating the entrance of natural light into the church interior by the hour,

he avoided the disturbing effect of direct sunlight during services by devising the exact design of the curves and gaps through daylight-simulation software. As a result, lighting remains indirect throughout the morning, with the first rays hitting the walls in the early afternoon, when the hymns are sung towards the end of mass. At around 3pm, light begins to pour in, while the curves dramatically enhance its brightness.

KORO HOUSE

TOYOTA, JAPAN
KATSUTOSHI SASAKI

This single-family house sits on a corner plot in a nondescript residential area. Architect Katsutoshi Sasaki moved it to the back of the plot and laid out a garden as a filter between the house and the two roads. Fortunately, the location afforded an unobscured view of the sky and ensured plenty of sunlight. 'I proposed to lift the roof off of the exterior wall, to take in the view of the sky and natural light from the whole circumference of the house,' Sasaki says. A series of wooden battens hanging from the roof into the full-height family room acts as a 'light reservoir', which reflects the transition of sunlight, 'letting the inhabitants feel the flux of time'.

HOUSE IN KOMAE

TOKYO, JAPAN
MAKOTO YAMAGUCHI, MAYUMI KONDO

The introverted nature of this design was dictated by the need to protect residents from future changes in the neighbourhood, including the replacement of old houses by modern apartment blocks. The lighting concept, developed by Makoto Yamaguchi with Mayumi Kondo, contributes to the serene atmosphere. The house has a series of double-height courtyards with white curved walls. These 'light courts' serve as lighting devices for the rooms, which are not equipped with any other fixtures. During the day, the curved walls direct sunlight into both storeys (ground and basement). At night, the house is illuminated by artificial lighting installed at the bottom of the reflector walls.

DAYLIGHT HOUSE

TOKYO, JAPAN
TAKESHI HOSAKA

One would hardly believe that this generously lit house, designed by Takeshi Hosaka for a family of four, is located in a dark 'urban valley' between closely packed buildings. The entire project was shaped by the desire to maximize natural light in a space that could only be lit from above. In this single-room arrangement, the sleeping zones are separated from the main living space by partitions that are half the height of the room. Twenty-nine skylights pierce the roof, each one screened with a bent sheet of white acrylic to help diffuse and soften the light. The distance between the skylights and the acrylic sections, along with the colours of the acrylic and the wood, are optimized to ensure uniform lighting. The name of the house refers to the beauty of the light as it changes over the course of a 24-hour cycle.

CLYFFORD STILL MUSEUM
DENVER, COLORADO
ALLIED WORKS ARCHITECTURE

The artist Clyfford Still, one of the central figures of Abstract Expressionism, believed that light made paintings come alive. The opening of the Clyfford Still Museum in Denver, Colorado, created a unique opportunity to see hundreds of never-before exhibited works by Still, as well as experience an almost physical presence of light, fused with and reflected by the museum's concrete ceiling. In a city that gets an average of 300 days of sunshine a year, the effect feels completely natural, yet it took the team from Allied Works Architecture and daylighting experts from Arup two years to develop a design solution that would determine what visitors would actually see and how to adjust it throughout the year. The gallery's ceiling is a 2.4 m (8 ft)-deep diffusion mechanism. Light enters through translucent skylights, is reflected off the white walls and further diffuses through three-dimensional apertures in the concrete ceiling. Tests performed on a life-size maquette proved that the final result (right) would be exactly as promised by the computer model (above).

ELEANOR AND HENRY HITCHCOCK CHARITABLE FOUNDATION GALLERY

UNDERHOUSE

YVELINES, FRANCE
PAUL COUDAMY

This proposal for a one-family house in the Paris region is also a potential response to a frequently occurring situation in urban contexts: a residential project that is surrounded tightly by other buildings. French architect Paul Coudamy proposed placing the entire house underground and illuminating it via a system of skylight tubes of varying sizes. According to Coudamy, the scheme combines several advantages, ensuring both natural light and privacy, as well as plenty of open-air space for the residents to enjoy.

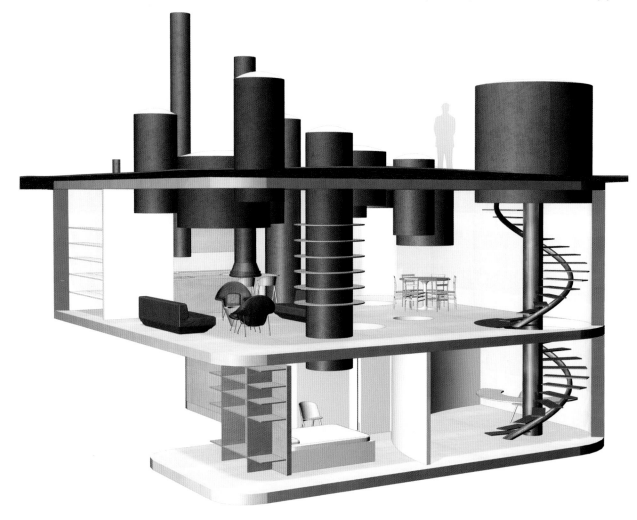

STÄDEL MUSEUM

FRANKFURT, GERMANY
SCHNEIDER + SCHUMACHER, LICHT KUNST LICHT

In developing the lighting concept for a
subterranean extension to the Städel Museum
in Frankfurt, architects Schneider+Schumacher
joined forces with Licht Kunst Licht and
Zumtobel. The self-supporting, elegantly curved
ceiling is punctured with 195 skylights, which are
the sources of both natural and artificial light,
as each is fitted with a ring of warm and cool-
white LEDs. Skylight modules can be individually
controlled to adapt the lighting conditions for the
different spaces and exhibits.

DAYLIGHT ENTRANCE, SUBCONSCIOUS EFFECTS OF DAYLIGHT, DAYLIGHT COMES SIDEWAYS

DANIEL RYBAKKEN

In this series of experiments Daniel Rybakken replicated natural light in its most common yet impactful manifestations. In Daylight Comes Sideways (opposite, bottom left), the effect of sunlight and shadows was simulated by placing individually dimmable LEDs behind a translucent surface. This was followed by Subconscious Effects of Daylight (opposite, right), in which a patch of light, complete with a realistic pattern of a shadow,

was projected onto the floor from beneath a table. Incorporated directly into the architecture itself, Daylight Entrance (above and opposite, top left) recreates the 'positive sensation of sunlight' in the windowless entrance hall of an office building. Spanning three floors, the illusion was created by 6,000 LEDs, which form light patterns on aluminium sheets concealed behind solid-surface wall panels.

WHITE LIGHT
PAUL COCKSEDGE

This installation, presented during a solo exhibition at the Friedman Benda gallery in New York, explored the complex nature of white light. The project consisted of an empty room with an illuminated ceiling that switched between two radically different colour modes, as its dense mosaic of rainbow-coloured tiles slowly faded into white. For visitors who did not look up, nothing would appear to change in the room, which seemed to be continually lit by natural light. The key lay in the precise calibration and positioning of the colour tiles, which produced a similar hue of warm white light; the slightest shift in the colour combination would have been enough to ruin the effect.

COELUX

PAOLO DI TRAPANI

CoeLux technology is the result of decade-long research, in which physicist Paolo Di Trapani sought to reproduce the atmospheric optical phenomena found in nature. The subtle details that signify the outdoors, such as the deep blue of the sky or the contrasting luminance of colour in light and shadow, are now available as an indoor experience. Intended for spaces that lack natural light, CoeLux modules comprise three key elements: LEDs that reproduce the sunlight spectrum; a sophisticated optical system that emulates the distance between the sky and the sun; and nanostructured materials, which recreate the Rayleigh scattering process that occurs in the atmosphere.

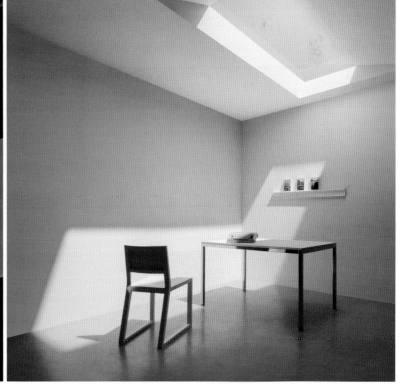

RHYTHM

DEVELOPING A MUTABLE HORIZON, ONE LINE DRAWING

CHRIS FRASER

Altering our perception of the most elementary and largely unnoticed phenomena, such as the daily cycle of sunlight or the way light enters a room, artist Chris Fraser makes sense of Oscar Wilde's observation about the true mystery of the world being the visible, and not the invisible. Both One Line Drawing (right) and Developing a Mutable Horizon (above) belong to a series of site-specific projects, in which Fraser uses the age-old camera obscura effect to create what he describes as 'focused spaces of physical presence'. For One Line Drawing,

he built a darkroom inside Mills College Art Museum, in Oakland, California, leaving a gap where one of the walls would have met the ceiling. 'This slit translated the gallery's ornate skylight into a linear image that contoured along the walls and floor of the space,' he explains, 'and changed rapidly over the course of the day.' A similar experience was created in Developing a Mutable Horizon, in which a single, strategically placed slit diffracted a mix of natural and electric light, heightening the viewer's awareness of both space and time.

MELT AND RECREATE

SIRI BAHLENBERG, SOFIA BERGFELDT

Constant transformation is the normal state for this ice lamp designed by Siri Bahlenberg and Sofia Bergfeldt. As the lampshade melts, water is collected in a mould placed beneath it. When all the ice has melted, the mould is put in the freezer to make a new lamp. Each moulding process is unique, which is why the endlessly recycled lamp will never look the same.

SWELL
PAUL COCKSEDGE

Inspired by the natural phenomena of
substances that expand and contract with
changes in temperature, Paul Cocksedge
designed the Swell lamp, in which the entire
cycle is reproduced with the help of an
incandescent bulb and its by-product: heat.
The lamp initially appears as a bubble of solid,
coloured glass; once it is switched on, the tinted
liquid inside the bubble warms up and gradually
expands, rising like mercury in a thermometer.

SURFACE TENSION LAMP
FRONT

By the time the LED burns out, the Surface
Tension Lamp, designed by Sofia Lagerkvist,
Charlotte von der Lancken and Anna Lindgren of
Swedish design trio Front, will have worn away
some three million soap-bubble lampshades.
'We wanted to create a constantly changing
lamp that combines the most ephemeral of
lampshades with a light source that will last for
50,000 hours,' say the designers.

LIGHT IN WATER
DORELL GHOTMEH TANE, IZUMI OKAYASU

Presented at Milan Design Week 2011 and recreated a few years later for the inaugural exhibition at the Éléphant Paname art and dance centre in Paris, this installation by architectural firm Dorell Ghotmeh Tane placed spellbound viewers in front of a sparkling shower, in which water drops appeared as particles of light, as rapid as they were distinct. For Éléphant Paname (home of the oldest concrete dome in Paris), the design was adapted to the hall's circular form, allowing visitors to step inside the ring of luminous rain. The water came from ceiling-mounted perforated tubes, with each hole emitting sixty drops per second. As for the magic, it was performed by the specially developed LED lighting time control system. Together with lighting designer Izumi Okayasu, the architects reduced the system's programmable on/off times to the shortest possible interval, an imperceptible 7 microseconds, which made it possible to visualize a single point of light in the water. When the lighting time was extended to 6,000 microseconds, the point of light transformed into a line.

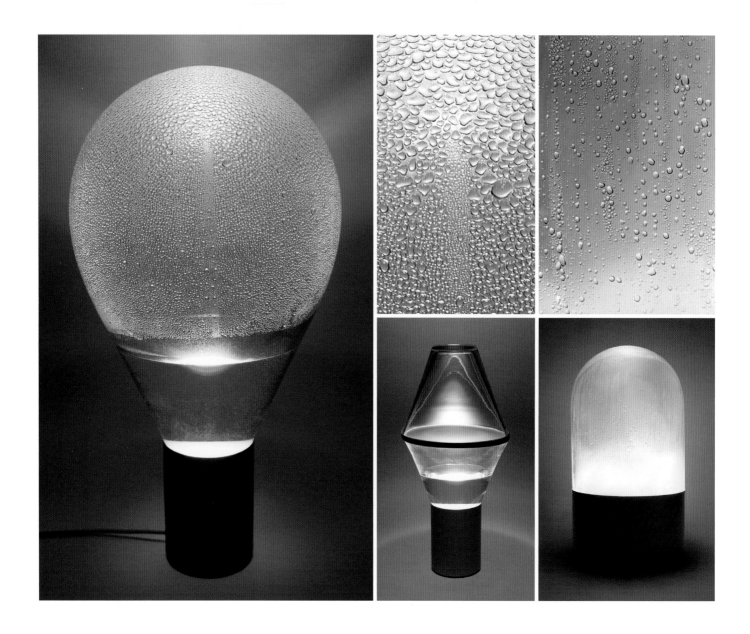

WATER LAMPS
ARTURO ERBSMAN

For this series of lamps, Arturo Erbsman visualized the flow of time by observing and highlighting different states of water. Water is sealed inside Atmos (above left) to loop the cycle of condensation. When the light is switched on, evaporating water condenses on the inner surface of the bulb, forming micro- droplets that diffuse light. The droplets merge, then slide back into the water reserve. Cumulus (above right), a 'personal cloud storage lamp', uses ultrasound to turn water into mist; Clepsydra (above middle) revisits ancient water clocks, while focusing on the beauty of illuminated ripples.

DAY & NIGHT LIGHT

ÉLÉONORE DELISSE

This proposed design solution for seasonal affective disorder helps rebalance our internal clock by providing the different colours of light our minds and bodies need over the course of a 24-hour cycle. A key component of the design is dichroic glass, which rotates in front of the lamp, projecting blue light in the mornings to stimulate wakefulness and a warm, relaxing amber glow in the evenings to activate the production of melatonin and send us to sleep.

HAFENCITY UNIVERSITÄT STATION

HAMBURG , GERMANY
RAUPACH ARCHITEKTEN, STAUSS + PEDRAZZINI,
PFARRÉ LIGHTING DESIGN

Raupach Architects teamed up with industrial designers Stauss + Pedrazzini and lighting expert Gerd Pfarré to redesign HafenCity Universität underground station. As a principal space-maker, light adds vibrancy to architecture through simple economic solutions. Twelve lightboxes, each the size of a standard shipping container, are suspended above the platform. Each 'container' incorporates RGB LEDs for colour-changing effects, while the area underneath the containers illuminates the platform with soft, white fluorescent light. The changing colours of light follow a cyclic pattern: chilly ultramarine blue during the day; warm orange at night; and colour signals that announce the arrival of trains. This luminous choreography is echoed by dark, reflective cladding, whose glare-free aspect heightens the value and energy of colour.

1 BEDROOM / 2 SHOWER / 3 WASH BASIN
4 KITCHEN / 5 DINING ROOM / 6 LIVING ROOM

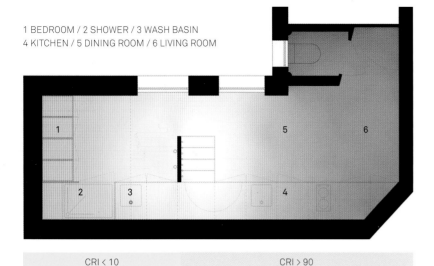

CRI < 10	CRI > 90

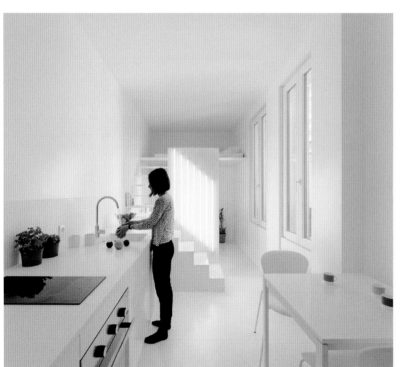

SPECTRAL APARTMENT

LEVALLOIS, FRANCE
NICOLAS DORVAL-BORY, RAPHAËL BÉTILLON

Insufficient natural light was the primary motivator behind the renovation of this 20 m² (215 sq ft) studio flat, so smart artificial lighting was central to the project. Architects Nicolas Dorval-Bory and Raphaël Bétillon found a solution when they looked to the colour-rendering index (CRI), a parameter normally neglected in residential architecture, which uses a 100-point scale to measure the ability of a light source to realistically show colours. (The familiar orange light of low-pressure sodium lamps, used in street lighting because of their energy efficiency, has a near-zero CRI, making it impossible to distinguish colours.) The architects created a 'bipolar' layout, in which different functional zones are grouped according to whether or not they required good colour rendering. A partition wall, 2 m (7 ft) high, divides the open-plan flat into two sections: the kitchen and living room, where it is more important to distinguish colours; and the bedroom and bathroom, where monochromatic light is sufficient. Fixed on one side of the wall are fluorescent tubes, which provide neutral 90+ CRI light; on the other side – the 'night zone' – low-pressure sodium lamps offer a warmer light with low CRI.

RAINBOW STATION

AMSTERDAM, NETHERLANDS
STUDIO ROOSEGAARDE

Every year, some 50 million people travel through
Amsterdam Centraal railway station. Throughout
2015, those fortunate enough not to be inside the
station an hour after sunset saw a giant rainbow
appear on the 45 m (148 ft)-wide roof. This
daily miracle was the result of a collaboration
between Dutch designer Daan Roosegaarde
and astronomers from the University of Leiden.
Together, they developed a lens filter for splitting
light into a spectrum of colours, while new
liquid crystal technology devised for exoplanet
research helped to fit the rainbow precisely into
the semicircular roof.

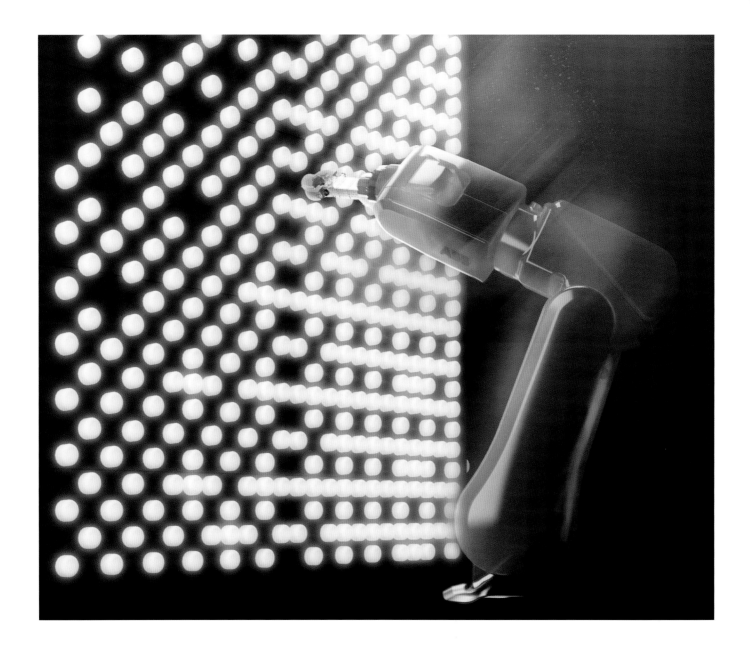

FREE PIXEL
CARLO RATTI

'Pixels will soon be liberated from screens to become tangible and controllable light particles,' says architect Carlo Ratti. With the invention and further development of LEDs, artificial light has evolved from a rigid infrastructure to a mobile and independent 'ecosystem', and from the 'on/off' mode to the capacity to create 'infinite gradients in space and time', or even 'three-dimensional displays, atomized and diffused into the air'. Under the aegis of Italian brand Artemide, Ratti has demonstrated the first steps towards the complete liberation of light: Free Pixel employs a robotic arm to manipulate an array of LED modules and produce an endless flow of random patterns.

VECTOR

COURBEVOIE, FRANCE
TRAFIK

The aim of this collaboration between media designers Trafik and Saazs, promoters of new-generation light sources, was to produce a digital wall for the French Patent Office. Containing fifty-four modules, the 702 illuminated glass sections provide a matrix for a dynamic display that allows for the transmission of alphanumeric messages and abstract patterns across the entire surface of the 10 × 4 m (33 × 15 ft) wall.

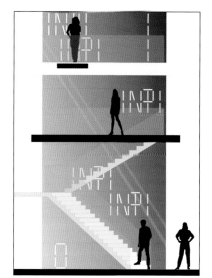
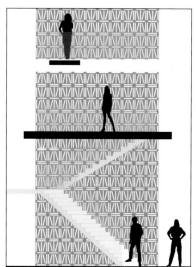

MULTIVERSE

WASHINGTON, DC
LEO VILLAREAL

For this project, American artist Leo Villareal sent
abstract configurations of moving light across
the dark underground passage that connects the
National Gallery of Art's East and West Buildings.
Villareal installed approximately 41,000 LED
nodes into the curved ceiling above a 61 m (200
ft)-long travelator. Custom-designed software
enables various sequences of the luminous
'pixels', which can be overlaid in multiple layers,
allowing for the creation of different effects in
accordance with which layers are switched on or
off. The infinitely changing light sculptures are
'communicating in some way', notes the artist,
but visitors are free to create their own meanings
out of these messages.

DIURNISME
PARIS, FRANCE
PHILIPPE RAHM

For the 'Airs de Paris' exhibition at the Pompidou Centre in 2007, Philippe Rahm flooded a room with light to create a typically nocturnal effect. His project looked back to the nineteenth century, when the introduction of street lighting revolutionized urban nightlife. In a counteract to 'creating the day during the night', Rahm's ambition was to 'physically produce the night during the day', achieving it with more contemporary and indirect means. 'After nocturnalism, I want to invent "diurnism", using bright orange-yellow light with wavelengths exceeding 570 nanometres,' he says. 'The human body responds to it by producing the same amount of the melatonin hormone as it does during the real night. The room becomes a paradox between the visual and the physiological: a night that looks like a bright day.'

SPLIT TIMES CAFÉ

LEIBLING, AUSTRIA
PHILIPPE RAHM

For this café at the FOC Eybesfeld, Philippe Rahm has continued his experiments in designing time through architecture, or rather, through the ways this architecture is illuminated. The café is divided into three zones, in which Rahm has created different 'physiological environments' that change the perception of time from natural to artificial night and day. The first area is enveloped in clear glass, which faithfully replicates the colours of natural light as it changes throughout the day. In the second, the glass envelope is blue. As blue light blocks the secretion of melatonin, this space is the 'perpetual day' zone, intended for shorter stays and more energetic activity. In the third and final zone, yellow glass helps to reproduce the physiological night. Wavelengths corresponding to the yellow part of the spectrum are melatonin-friendly, so here the designer has set up a chill-out area with space and seating for lounging.

BLUE SKY LAMP

CHRIS KABEL

Blue light has been proven to have a calming effect and to boost our ability to concentrate. Conceived for the Winter Anti-Depression Show at the contemporary culture centre Marres in Maastricht, Blue Sky Lamp is a mood-enhancing tool that recreates the light of the sky on a sunny day. Titanium oxide nano-powder contained in the transparent resin filter scatters the light of the LED in the same way the earth's atmosphere scatters the light from the sun.

PHASES, LUNAIRE

FERRÉOL BABIN

With Phases (below) and Lunaire (right), two lamps created by French designer Ferréol Babin, all it takes is a single push/pull gesture to produce a personal eclipse. The light source is fitted into a large, circular diffuser and covered with a black disc. When placed in front of the diffuser, the lamp emits powerful, neutral light, but when the black disc is pushed inwards, the light source is shifted behind the diffuser, switching the lamp to backlighting mode.

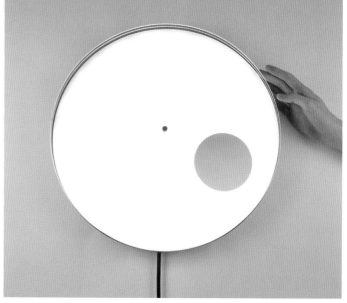

SYZYGY SERIES

OS&OOS

In astronomy, the term 'syzygy' refers to a straight-line configuration of three celestial bodies, and is often used in relation to the sun, the earth and the moon. Here, a circular light source and a set of filtering discs are used to mimic three different aspects of the syzygy: transit (right), occultation (above left) and eclipse (above right). Like the sun, the light source is always on, and its brightness can only be adjusted by blocking it, partially or completely.

THANKS FOR THE SUN,
THANKS FOR THE PLANETS

ARNOUT MEIJER

The perception of different colour temperatures
and the transition between warm and cool light
are the defining factors of Arnout Meijer's series
of luminous sculptures. Thanks for the Sun
(below) helps users recreate the varying warmth
and intensity of light over the course of a 24-hour
cycle in a world where the bright, unchanging
light of electronic screens accompanies us
throughout the day. Thanks for the Planets (right)
is a series of four objects that use fine linear
patterns to create atmospheric mixes of white
and coloured light.

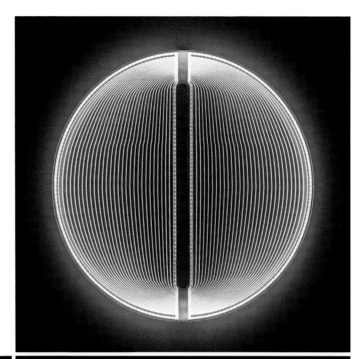

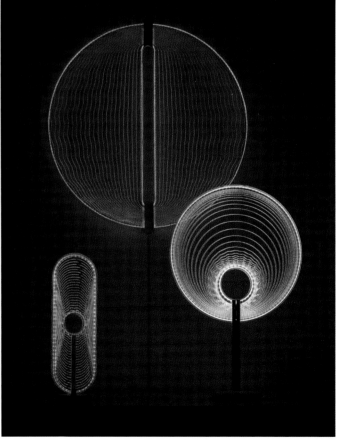

MOMENTUM

Designed for The Curve, a 90 m (295 ft)-long gallery space at the Barbican Centre, this project fuses movement, sound and light into an immersive experience that alters perceptions of time and physical space to heighten consciousness of both. Inspired by the Foucault pendulum, which demonstrates the rotation of the earth, the team at United Visual Artists decided to 'recreate the experiment while taking control of it', as Ben Kreukniet explains. Using the gallery's curved space as a canvas, the artists transformed it into a 'spatial instrument' that consists of twelve mechanical pendulums with a speaker and a light source incorporated into each bob (the weight on the end of a pendulum). A mechanism controls the swinging patterns, which range from natural to 'synthesized' and seemingly anomalous. Enhancing the sense of space, the sources of sound sway together with the pendulums, while moving light points project shadows and planes of light across the 6 m (20 ft)-high walls and the curved floor.

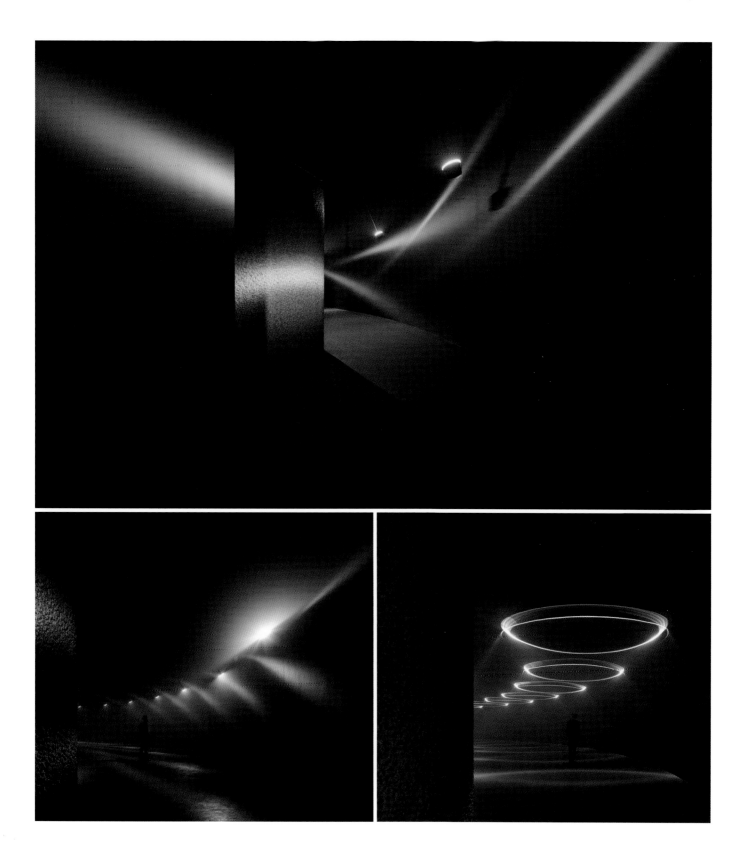

SHADE

LONDON, UK
SIMON HEIJDENS

Artist Simon Heijdens covered the curved glass façade (140 m², or 1,507 sq ft) of the NOW Gallery with an intelligent skin whose cells transform from opaque to clear in response to the ever-changing patterns of wind (opposite). The project 'restored the unplanned natural timeline of the outdoors to the interior of the building,' says Heijdens, as it 'filtered natural sunlight into a moving kaleidoscope of light and shadow, choreographed by the elements passing outside.'

ENDLESS

BRAM VANDERBEKE

This luminous device by Belgian designer Bram Vanderbeke (below) was designed to capture nothing less than infinity. A moveable mirror in translucent acrylic is set inside a thick, circular frame fitted with LED lights, while combined light- and mirror-effects generate continually changing infinite reflections. Cast resin used for the frame adds a cloudy touch to this metaphorical 'container for the future'.

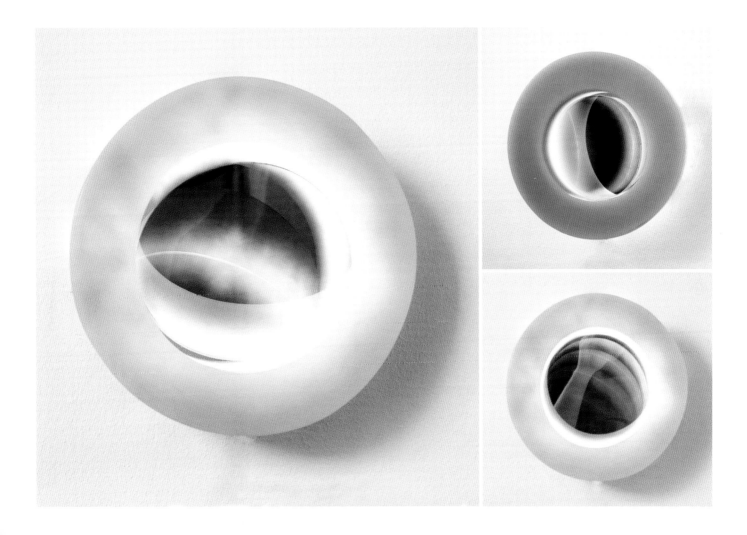

RIPPLE
POETIC LAB

These lamps by Hanhsi Chen and Shikai Tseng of
London-based design studio Poetic Lab (above)
heighten the beauty of blown glass through light
and motion. A constantly changing pattern of
light and shadow is created by slowly rotating an
irregularly shaped glass dome, lit from within.

POLARIS, LOUMINOUS ALCHEMY
LAURENT FORT

A light source mounted on a flexible stem and a
piece of moulded polycarbonate form the basic
toolkit for Laurent Fort's space-transforming
'sculptures of light'. Polaris (opposite, top) aims to
reproduce the mesmerizing colour modulations
of the Aurora Borealis with a sheet of iridescent
polycarbonate, rotating at a pace of 1 rpm.
In Louminous Alchemy (opposite, bottom), a
series of light effects are produced by manually
adjusting the position of the lamp.

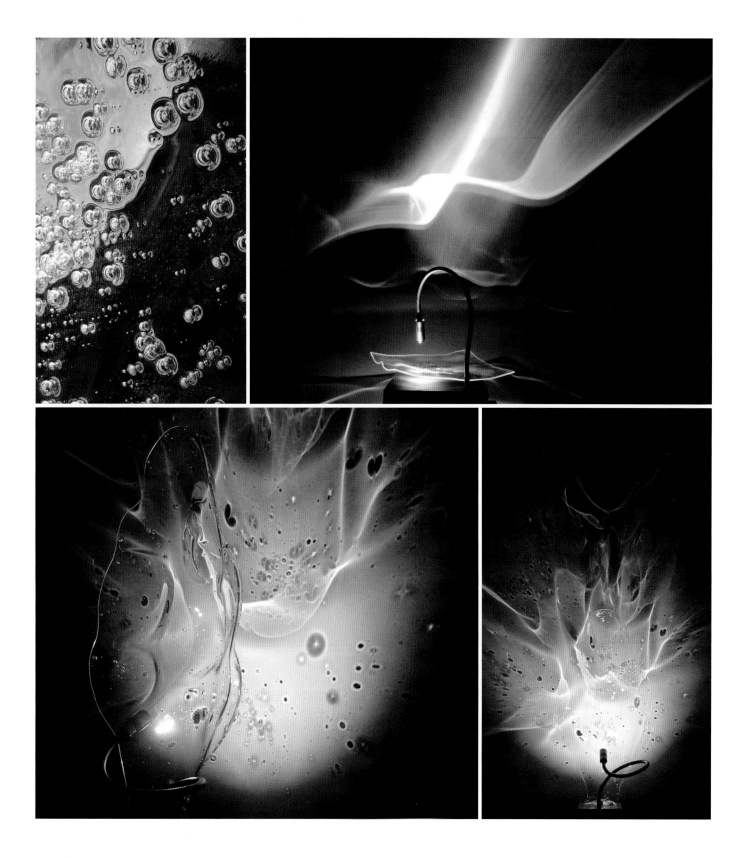

TRANSFORMING

EMOTION

Perhaps one of the most profound effects of the new technologies is that they expand our perception and offer new ways of experiencing the world. Bauhaus visionary László Moholy-Nagy wrote in *Vision in Motion* (1946) about the importance of bringing an individual's intellectual and emotional perception into a balanced whole in order to 'arrive at an integrated life in which he would function to the fullest of his capacities through . . . the coordination of penetrative thinking and profound feeling. To reach this goal,' he continued, 'to feel what we know and know what we feel, is one of the tasks of our generation.'

Moholy-Nagy considered the role of artists in our 'emotionally illiterate' society particularly important as it was their duty 'to penetrate yet-unseen ranges of the biological functions, to search the new dimensions of the industrial society and to translate the new findings into emotional orientation'.

In the ever-relevant process of emotional activation, light(ing) is a major player. The activation process may start with 'acupunctural' experiences, such as those presented in this chapter's 'Intensity' section. From the careful orchestration of shadows performed by artec3 Studio in their lighting scheme for a showroom for Lagares (p. 182) to luminaries elevated to the role of space-makers in projects by Mathieu Lehanneur (p. 186) and .PSLAB (p. 187), from the application of state-of-the-art technology to reproduce the flicker of the candle flame to the distortion of neon tubes and seeing what happens to the light, design intelligence is used to provoke vivid emotional responses.

Colour is another key factor in creating an emotional impact. Discovering the effects of colour on our physical and psychological state has been an object of both scientific and artistic research for a long time now. The section 'Colour

Power' draws from both realms, demonstrating light as a potent and flexible tool in the design of different colour-based scenarios. New opportunities are afforded by LED technology. The colour of light produced by each chip depends on the material of its semiconductor, allowing the creation of a spectrum that can be analysed, broken up and redesigned, combining specific wavelengths to achieve certain colour effects in a way reminiscent of the technique used by Impressionist artists. We are again reminded of Moholy-Nagy's future-orientated ideas, notably his experiments with light and motion in an attempt to 'discard brush and pigment and to "paint" by means of light itself'.

In 'Interaction', the artworks featured appeal to emotions in a different way. There is much more to these designs than pushing the on/off button: they require a different kind of involvement from their owners, who are encouraged to fold and unfold; slide and adjust; touch and push, as they explore everything these devices have to offer. Light installations that react to sound, heat and motion engage in a dialogue with users, respond to the changing weather and emulate the behaviour of living organisms.

And finally, the designs in 'Immersion' are the outcome – or destination? – of research in which art and architecture, optics and physiology, intellect and curiosity, the natural and machine-made, luminescence and illumination converge to produce environments where seeing, feeling and thinking form an organic whole.

INTENSITY

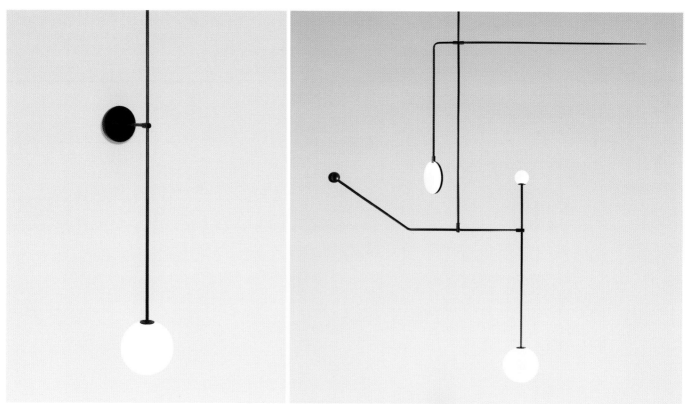

MOBILE CHANDELIERS

MICHAEL ANASTASSIADES

London-based designer Michael Anastassiades
claims that he doesn't think about luminaires
as physical objects, as he believes they have
to work in a different dimension. His series of
kinetic chandeliers, which has been evolving
since 2008, integrates light into visually and
physically balanced spatial compositions with
finely calibrated geometries.

MOBILE LIGHT

KOUICHI OKAMOTO

Designed by Kouichi Okamoto, the creative force
behind Japanese label Kyouei Design, this kinetic
sculpture is formed from solar-powered LED
modules that switch on automatically when the
surrounding space darkens.

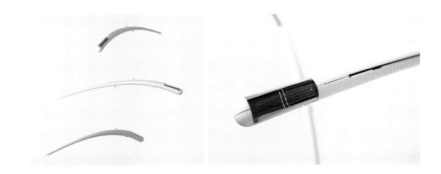

FLYING FLAMES

MORITZ WALDEMEYER, INGO MAURER

This joint project by Moritz Waldemeyer and Ingo Maurer faithfully recreates the experience of looking at a candle flame. Pairing a bare circuit board featuring the latest in microprocessor technology with 256 high-quality LEDs per candle, says Waldemeyer, 'is all it takes to evoke the natural flow and flicker'. For a truly life-like effect, the duo processed video footage of a real candle with a random algorithm to ensure that the sequence of movements never repeats. The result is shown on an LED display, the colour of which has been matched exactly to that of a candle flame.

LED ON FIRE
BART LENS

In this pendant luminaire incorporating an LED module and a wax candle, Belgian architect and lighting designer Bart Lens explores the coexistence of two radically different light sources: LED lights and an open fire. The LED source remains invisible, yet the light emitted shines through the layer of wax.

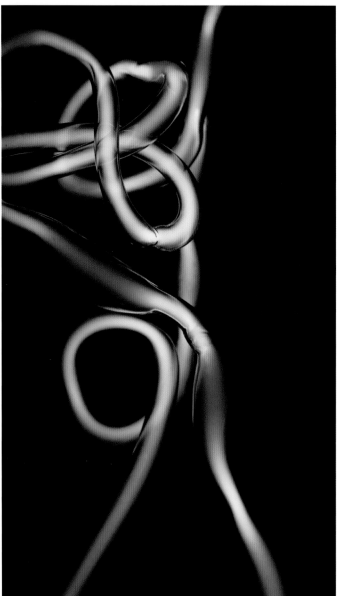

PHENOMENEON
PIEKE BERGMANS

Going against the received wisdom that only a straight neon tube can produce light, designer Pieke Bergmans used existing glass-processing methods to create spherical or wildly free-form tubes for her Phenomeneon series, an exploration of the behaviour of light. She discovered that neon would only light up in the narrow segments of the tubes, disappearing when the vessel widens. 'The gas remains in motion,' she says, 'but not always visible, as if it were alive' – the name, in fact, of one of the pieces in the series (left and bottom).

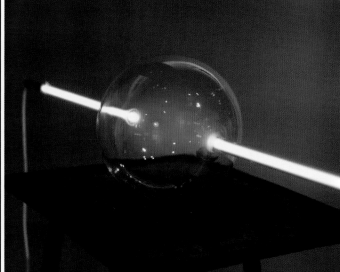

FROM THE SKY
PIEKE BERGMANS

Now part of the collection of the Groninger Museum, From the Sky (below) is from Bergmans's Light Blubs series, in which she has applied her signature 'design virus' approach to a traditional light bulb. The artist collaborated with factories to use conventional production techniques (here, glass-blowing) in new and extraordinary ways. Instead of creating precisely determined shapes, Bergmans prefers to limit her control over the process and allow the objects to evolve organically, similar to life forms that adapt to their environment as they grow.

VAPOR
PIEKE BERGMANS

First presented during Dutch Design Week 2013, these luminous objects emerged from one of the designer's numerous experiments in stretching the limits of industrial manufacturing techniques. In the Vapor series (above), Bergmans blew air through PVC tubes to create ghost-like mono-material shapes: solid on top, to thin and billowing at the bottom, before 'fading away into nothingness, almost like gas'.

COLLECTION OF LIGHT;
LIGHT CULTURE;
LIGHT ON GROUND

HUMANS SINCE 1982

Designers Per Emanuelsson and Bastian Bischoff of Stockholm-based studio Humans Since 1982 state that they are 'interested in the interest itself'. They mix concepts and methods from radically different realms 'to arouse fundamental curiosity by creating material hints of how the world might be'. In pursuing their creative research along these lines, the pair designed an aesthetically and politically charged chandelier composed of surveillance cameras, and used seventy-year-old insect-collection boxes to arrange different 'species' of tiny LEDs (each labelled with its name, size and colour temperature) into the limited-edition luminaire Collection Of Light (above and opposite, bottom right). Other projects also treat LEDs as micro-organisms, and include Light Culture (opposite, bottom left and top right) and Light On Ground (opposite, top left and middle right), the latter emphasizing the contrast between the illuminants' size and brightness by placing some eighty LEDs at the bottom of a 2 m (6 ft 6 in.)-tall container and filling the rest of the box with light.

PYRAMID
AQUA GALLERY

The precise geometry, articulated structure and sheer size that turn Pyramid, a series of bespoke light objects, into architectural elements are all rooted in the desire to create a strong emotional impact. Albi Serfaty, co-founder and art director of Aqua Gallery, says: 'Since every space needs to be filled with emotional content, I think about the feelings I would like to experience in an architectural space.' Everything from the impressive crystal chandeliers at La Scala opera house in Milan to an old Cartier watch found in the street, whose diamonds give off a special kind of glow when the lights at the cinema are dimmed, have changed Serfaty's way of looking at light. 'For me, the magical process of turning on a lamp and then dimming it is one of the biggest joys in lamp-making,' he says. 'I think of a kid standing in this space and looking at this lamp in wonder and joy. Once this feeling is achieved, I'll know I've done something right.'

FRAGILE FUTURE III

STUDIO DRIFT

Dandelion heads recomposed, seed by seed, stand in for nature in this installation representing the poetic fusion of technology and the natural world – the vision of Lonneke Gordijn and Ralph Nauta of Studio Drift for the future of the planet. Technology is symbolized by LEDs connected by three-dimensional electronic circuits to form modular structures adaptable to all kinds of applications, from freestanding objects to chandeliers or wall-mounted fixtures. With the seeds hand-glued onto them, LEDs mutate into light-emitting 'dandelights'. The project, 'a clear statement against mass production and throwaway culture', contemplates the possibility of natural evolution and technological development cross-pollinating each other in the future.

COLOUR BY NUMBERS

TOKYO, JAPAN
JAMO ASSOCIATES

A total of 162 fluorescent lamps shine from the ceiling of the Colour By Numbers fashion store, designed by Tokyo-based architectural firm Jamo. The domination of the colour white is one of the key elements in the concept for the interior design. The exceptional brightness of light – stronger even than the illumination in a convenience store – heightens the 'tension that exists in pure whiteness'.

LAGARES SHOWROOM

OLOT, SPAIN
RCR ARQUITECTES, ARTEC3 STUDIO

When developing the lighting concept for a showroom in Olot, Spain, design firm artec3 Studio drew inspiration from Japanese gardens, in which rocks, moss and sand form a unified space that radiates 'peace and elegant simplicity'. For a similar effect, the team treated shadows as essential attributes of the objects on display, achieved via a combination of spotlights arranged in lines and halogen lamps with a very narrow beam, all of which illuminate the products from above and cast a shadow directly beneath each one. Neatly ordered shadows enhance the sense of levitation, already present in the showroom design by RCR Arquitectes, who suspended individual pieces on tensioned steel threads. The minimalist approach to colour and materials (concrete for the ceiling, walls and floor; products in white porcelain) added to the zen-like quality of the space.

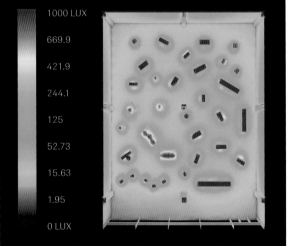

1000 LUX

669.9

421.9

244.1

125

52.73

15.63

1.95

0 LUX

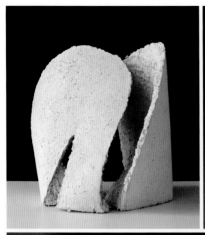

CHASMAL LUMEN
TAEG NISHIMOTO

Chasmal Lumen (left), a sculptural light object by architect and designer Taeg Nishimoto, is composed of two freestanding parts made of papercrete, a mix of repulped paper fibre and Portland cement. Smooth and convex on the outside, heavily textured and concave on the inside, the artwork conceals a light source and generates subtle, highly nuanced light and shadow projections that look exactly like ink-wash paintings.

YORUNOMA BAR
OSAKA, JAPAN
NAOYA MATSUMOTO

Led by architect Naoya Matsumoto, a team of young designers joined forces with local residents to fit out a pop-up bar (opposite) inside the 21 m² (226 sq ft) space of the Abenoma gallery in Osaka, Japan. The entire room was covered with crumpled tracing paper: 'It is fun to crumple paper, and anybody can do it,' says Matsumoto. Along with a few strategically placed light bulbs, this common but rarely used material transformed a neutral room into a mysteriously snug, grotto-like nook.

ELECTRIC

PARIS, FRANCE
MATHIEU LEHANNEUR, ANA MOUSSINET

Clusters of sound and lighting equipment
are suspended from the ceiling in this day
and night venue designed by Mathieu Lehanneur,
together with architect Ana Moussinet.
Spotlights appear to 'grow' off the crowns
of giant 'trees', whose massive trunks
are, in fact, plaits of electric cabling.

THE JANE

ANTWERP, BELGIUM
PIET BOON, .PSLAB

The design for the interior of The Jane, a restaurant located in the chapel of a former military hospital, is a collaboration between lighting experts from Beirut-based .PSLAB and architect Piet Boon. The focus of the lighting scheme is the dramatic 800 kg (1,764 lbs), 12 × 9 m (39 × 30 ft) chandelier, designed to 'contribute to the ambient divinity of the chapel interior'. A total of 150 metal rods, topped by LED bulbs, bristle in all directions, filling the vaulted void above the dining area and visible from the restaurant and the upper-level bar. Suspended 2.8 m (9 ft) above the floor, the chandelier defines a space that is highly impactful as well as intimate.

BAZAR NOIR

BERLIN, GERMANY
HIDDEN FORTRESS

For a concept store featuring unique objects, home accessories and books for design addicts, the architects from Hidden Fortress created a two-storey interior in which the main space is painted a uniform black, while the more intimate mezzanine is clad entirely in maritime pine plywood. The two levels are linked by a suspended 'stairbox', whose surface treatment interlocks those of the two contrasting environments. The lighting concept helped the design team make the most of this contrast. The extra-matte black paint used for the ground floor absorbs most of the diffused light that comes from inside and out, while precisely directed spotlights highlight the merchandise and prevent any unwanted shadows. In the mezzanine, with its more domestic feel, the warmth radiating from the wooden walls is accentuated by an indirect light source behind the panelling. As in a real home, the lamps on display become part of the lighting scheme.

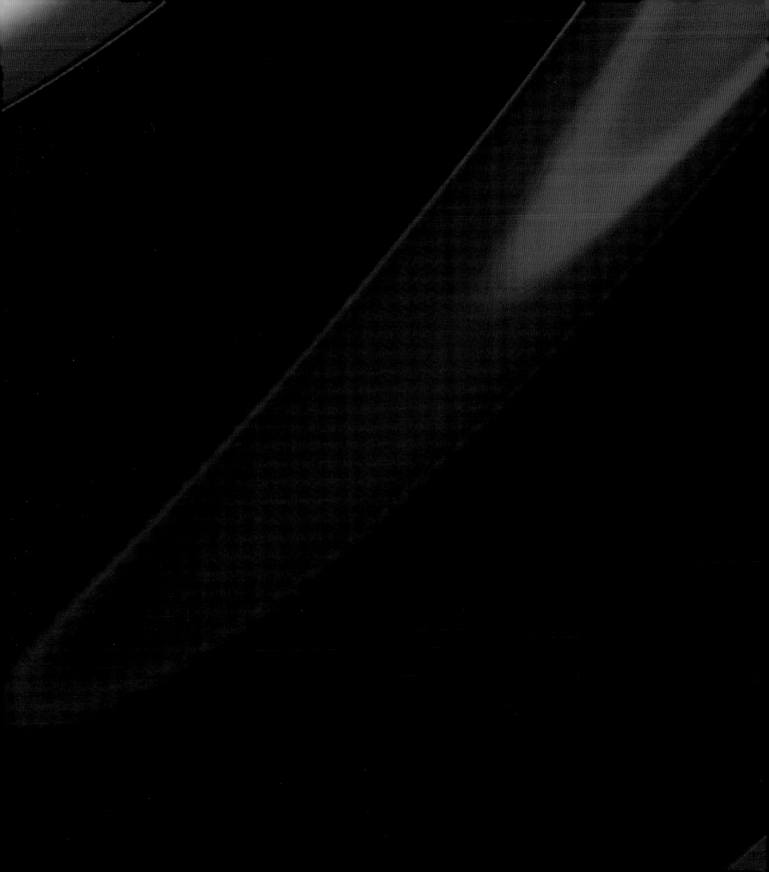

COLOUR POWER

HORIZON
FLYNN TALBOT

Designer Flynn Talbot wanted to recreate that twilight feeling, 'where the sun sets and the landscape is dark, but there is still a gradient of colour in the sky'. Scalable to fit into different locations, Horizon features colour-changing LED modules behind a stretch membrane, which ensures a smooth and evenly diffused light and conceals 'the technology and superfluous detail, so that one gets absorbed in the work'. Visitors are invited to colour-mix their own sunsets by controlling the artwork via a dedicated website.

SKY, LIGHT MAIL

ASTRID KROGH

In the best Danish design tradition, Astrid Krogh combines modern technology with traditional craftsmanship to produce such luminous textile works as the Sky series (above), in which optic fibres are woven from paper yarn on a loom. Connected to monitors, the optic fibre warps transmit slowly evolving, iridescent sequences across the entire piece. This 'breathing light' effect is particularly captivating in large-scale works including the 16 m (52 ft 6 in.)-tall Light Mail (right), which animates the lightwell of the 21C Museum Hotel in Cincinnati, Ohio.

SHIFTING LUMINOSITY
LIZ WEST

British artist Liz West uses colour theory and light fields to transform architectural spaces into sensory experiences. This 'spatial drawing' is an array of black pipes, balanced against white walls, which emit bursts of light from their undersides. The resulting fields of luminous colour gently mix on the borders, while the pipes, sagging under their own weight, stitch the whole picture together with huge graphic 'strokes'. An important detail is that the source of light is never truly exposed, but instead hinted at.

MIRAGE

GIORGIA ZANELLATO

Seduced by the chromatic richness and soft yet
powerful glow of neon signs, Italian designer
Giorgia Zanellato applied the unique qualities
of neon to a series of lamps and illuminated
mirrors. Called Mirage, the collection owes
its impact to the contrast between the iconic
geometries dominated by curved neon tubes and
the ethereal halos of coloured light cast on the
surrounding surfaces.

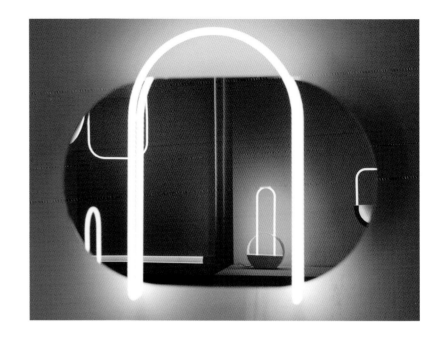

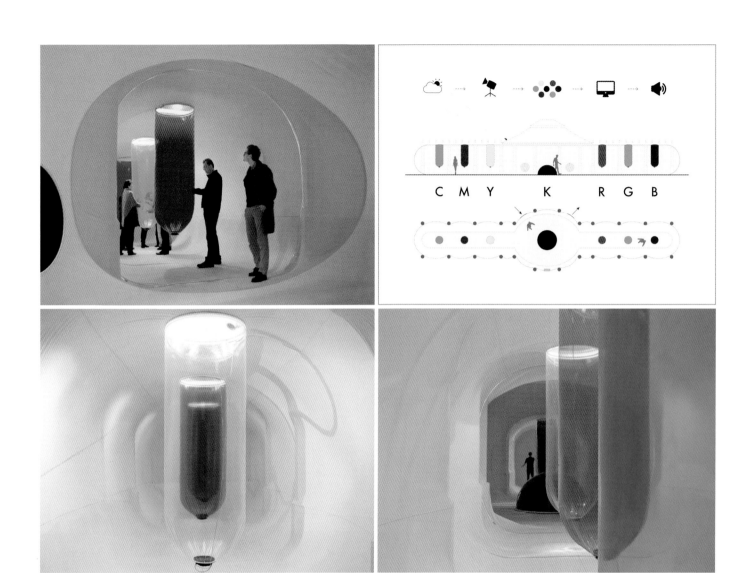

SOUND OF LIGHT
PLASTIQUE FANTASTIQUE, MARCO BAROTTI

Citing neuroscientist Mriganka Sur, who argues that half of the human brain is devoted directly or indirectly to vision, the creators of the Sound of Light installation encourage us to take one step further and 'imagine hearing the colours we perceive'. To make this possible, Berlin-based Plastique Fantastique teamed up with sound designer Marco Barotti to set up an inflatable pavilion in which sunlight is 'interpreted and dynamically transformed into audio frequencies'. Presented at Urban Lights Ruhr 2014, the installation had a roof-mounted digital camera that filmed the sky and separated the image into six colours according to the primary RGB and secondary CMY colour models. Six hanging columns of corresponding colours received different frequencies and converted them into audio output; the woofers fixed to the bottom of each column transformed the pavilion into one giant vibrating loudspeaker.

COLOUR

DANIEL RYBAKKEN, ANDREAS ENGESVIK

Daniel Rybakken and Andreas Engesvik designed
this luminaire as an experiment in layering
colours and shapes, as well as in deconstructing
a lamp into several independent objects that can
be assembled in different ways. Users are invited
to place sheets of coloured glass in front of a
light source, which itself is screened by a flat,
opaque shade.

SUSTAINABLE

LUMINOUS TEXTILE, ONESPACE

PHILIPS LIGHTING, KVADRAT SOFT CELLS

Luminous Textile was born from an encounter between two brands: one keen to combine its LED technology with textiles; the other in search of a lighting partner to integrate LEDs into their textile-based acoustic panels. The combined expertise of Philips and Kvadrat gave rise to a unique architectural product that fuses ambient lighting, sound absorption, surface decoration and a dynamic image display. Seamlessly integrated into walls and ceilings, luminous textile panels contain multicolour LED modules, fixed to acoustic foam at 6 cm (2½ in.) intervals. Such an arrangement of LEDs is well suited for a low-resolution screen, a powerful instrument for 'bringing spaces alive'. A diffusion layer sandwiched between the LEDs and the external textile layer ensures high image quality. With the panels designed so that the source of light remains invisible, the OneSpace luminous ceiling, with a uniform white glow that emulates natural daylight, became the next logical step in the evolution of 'large luminous surfaces'.

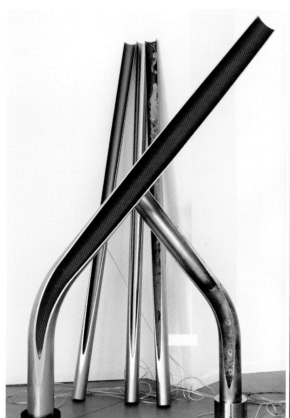

CONTRAST

JULIEN CARRETERO

For this series, designer Julien Carretero juxtaposes weight, colour, texture and light to reveal the inherent characteristics of metals such as brass, copper, bronze, aluminium and stainless steel. This is achieved by transforming industrial pipes into lighting objects with discreetly integrated LEDs. CNC-milled, laser-cut or handcrafted openings reveal the insides of the pipes. A variety of treatments, from lacquering, anodizing and brushing to the application of patinas or allowing natural oxidation, reinforces the tension between the contrasting surfaces.

SCRITTURA

CARLOTTA DE BEVILACQUA, LAURA PESSONI

Scrittura represents the third generation of systems for which Italian manufacturer Artemide focused on the high-precision rendering of light colour temperatures, with particular attention given to the nuances of white light, from warm yellow-orange to cold blue tones. The design of the basic linear modules enhances the architectural spaces with crisp and luminous, three-dimensional graphic elements. Its latest version can be remote-controlled through a series of simple gestures.

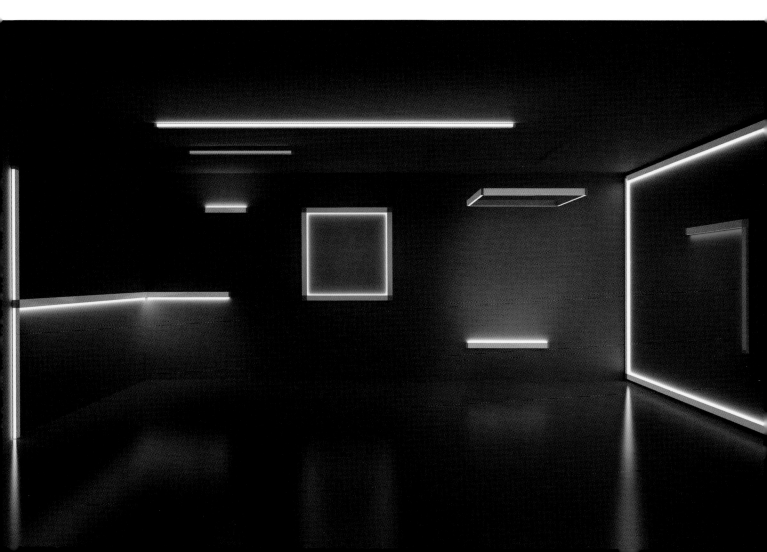

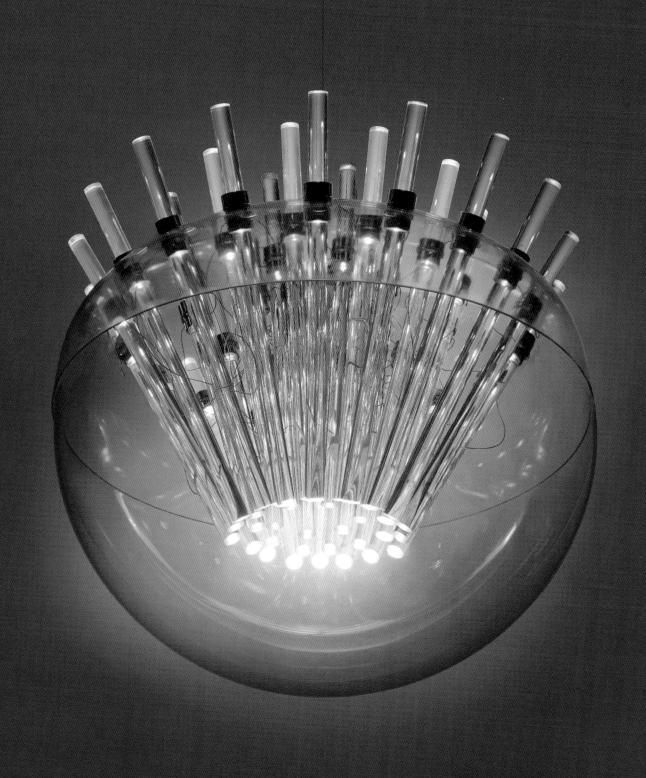

SPECTRAL LIGHT

PHILIPPE RAHM

VIOLET DEEP BLUE BLUE CYAN GREEN LIME ORANGE RED RED DEEP RED

Philippe Rahm describes his design method as breaking down the reality into 'elementary particles', such as wavelengths, humidity, light intensity, heat-transfer coefficients, and so on, and recomposing them into new forms that better respond to our needs, as well as to issues of energy efficiency and climate change. This approach reflects the latest developments in the lighting industry, in which the evolution of LEDs has made it possible to focus on designing the light spectrum itself, as each LED chip emits light at a particular wavelength. It also reflects the research interests of lighting brand Artemide,

one of the pioneers in the exploration of the psychological and physiological effects of light. For Artemide, Rahm designed Spectral Light, handpicking wavelengths that are beneficial for humans, their pets and their plants. Each wavelength is represented by an individual LED tube, or 'artificial ray'. Thirty-six such rays are gathered in a glass globe, in which their upper parts are visible as distinct colours, while the lower sections combine in the globe's translucent segment to merge, by way of colour addition, into the near-white spectrum of sunlight.

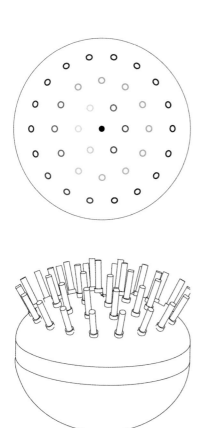

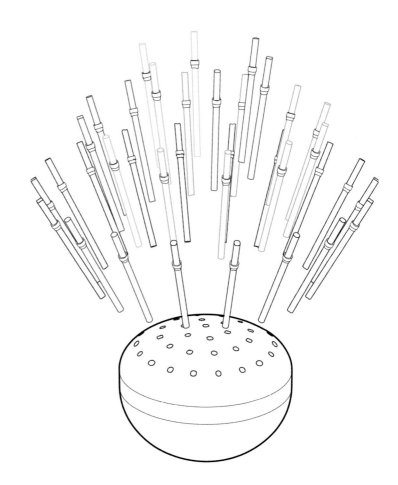

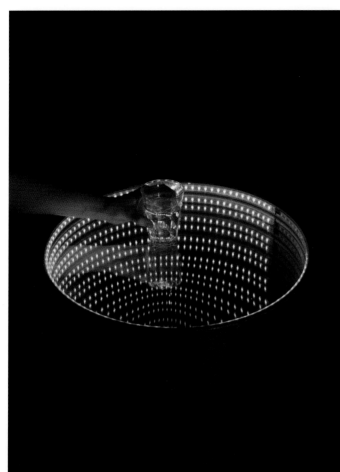

MERCURE LAMP
LUCIE LE GUEN

Inspired by mercury tilt switches, in which liquid mercury is used to activate or interrupt the electric circuit, the LED-powered Mercure Lamp (below) by French designer Lucie Le Guen is switched on and off when the blown-glass lamp, with its metallic beads that take on the role of mercury, is tilted.

INFINITUM
LOUISE-ANNE VAN 'T RIET

This table design by Louise-Anne van 't Riet (above) is a gentle, and aesthetically uplifting, reminder for those who tend to scatter their belongings. An infinite tunnel of luminous dots lights up each time something is placed on the table, and goes off when the objects are removed. The effect is produced by a combination of two mirrors with a strip of RGB LEDs and a piezo sensor switch that converts vibration to voltage.

RECTO-VERSO
BINA BAITEL

The intuitively controlled Recto-Verso
lamp (right) by French designer Bina Baitel
pairs organic light-emitting diode (OLED)
technology with the smart cover of an iPad.
Electroluminescent plaques are integrated in a
leather sheath, so that the lamp produces direct
light when the OLED side is rolled up, or ambient
light when the sheath is pulled down.

VIEWPOINT
CHUDY AND GRASE

Viewpoint (left) by Copenhagen-based design
duo Nils Chudy and Jasmina Grase 'plays tricks
with our sight', as its one-way mirror slides
along a backlit panel covered with a black-to-
white gradient pattern. One-way glass can only
function as a mirror when one of its sides is
brightly lit and the other is dark. With Viewpoint,
a reflection will be clearly visible when the mirror
is on the black side, gradually dissolving as it
moves towards the panel's luminous end.

IPPARCO

NEIL POULTON

Named after Hipparchus of Nicaea (Ipparco in Italian), the great astronomer and mathematician of Ancient Greece, a table lamp designed for Artemide (below) emits a halo of LED-based light from its head-ring. A magnet built into the ring gives this task light unprecedented mobility, as it allows for sliding the light source freely along and around the stem, or any other steel surface.

RICOCHET LIGHT

DANIEL RYBAKKEN

With the LED-based Ricochet Light (above), artist and designer Daniel Rybakken continues his investigations into the concept of an 'exploded lamp', formed not just by multiple components, but also by multiple objects. This allowed Rybakken to create a highly interactive object that encourages users to manipulate its individual parts – two pivoting mirrors and a diffuser – to adjust and redirect the light.

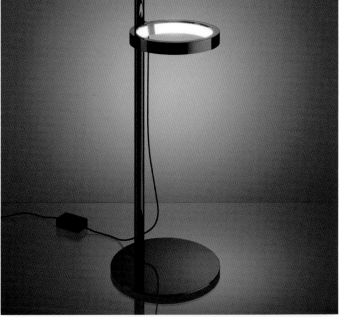

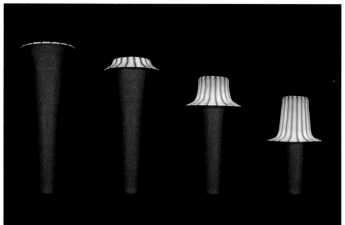

FRAGMENT

FERRÉOL BABIN

In his design for the Fragment lamp (below), French designer Ferréol Babin complements a light source with a series of small, tilted mirrors, which reflect and multiply the light that comes from a single point. 'By moving and turning the freestanding mirrors,' he explains, 'rays of light can reach almost anywhere in the room.'

PULL OVER

BINA BAITEL

Product and furniture designer Bina Baitel applies the casual act of adjusting a turtleneck sweater to a floor lamp, whose light output is controlled by a similar gesture. The inner surface of the Pull Over (above) is made from silicone-protected woven optical fibres, which distribute light from LEDs incorporated into its base, while the outer surface is coated with opaque silicone. The user is invited to modulate the light intensity, together with the shape of the lamp, by pulling down its flared end.

ALONE AT WORK

REGENT LIGHTING

Swiss manufacturer Regent Lighting developed
a smart system that offers its users both
psychological comfort and energy efficiency. The
product name speaks for itself: Alone at Work is
aimed at those who have to work late, remaining
in an empty, open-plan office in the dark. When
only one workspace is lit, feelings of loneliness
and isolation can creep in, while simply leaving
multiple fixtures switched on is not the best
solution in terms of energy-saving or efficiency.
As a kind of light therapy, the project's technology
uses a health-friendly, opto-electronic
connection to create a network of freestanding
luminaires that communicate with each other
and adjust their lighting mode to transform
solitary 'islands of light' into more pleasant 'light
clouds' with soft borders.

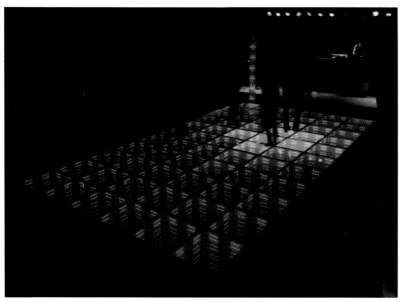

SUSTAINABLE DANCE FLOOR
STUDIO ROOSEGAARDE

Rotterdam-based design lab Studio Roosegaarde
and Sustainable Dance Club joined forces to
create the world's first human-powered dance
floor, which uses an electromechanical system
to convert the kinetic energy of revellers into
electricity. The brief was to design the top layer
of the floor to maximize the festive experience,
while expending as little energy as possible.
A combination of glass, mirrors and LEDs did
the job through colour-changing 'infinity effects'.
The light show is powered exclusively by the
movements of the dancers.

DISCO DISCO

ALEX ASSEILY, HABERDASHERY

The process of transforming the humble disco ball into
a sound-reactive light sculpture required the joint effort
of several London-based creative minds. Initiated by
entrepreneur Alex Asseily and 'kickstarted, design-wise'
by Goodwin Hartshorn consultancy, the project was
then developed in earnest by art-meets-design studio
Haberdashery. Programmed to respond to all kinds of audio
input, from a soundtrack to visitor feedback, and 'a gentle
blown kiss to a primordial scream', the system converts
sounds into visual patterns. A thick crown of elaborately
shaped acrylic fins transmits and amplifies the light, so that
it fills the entire space.

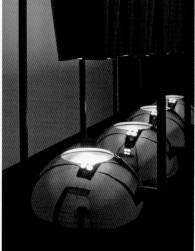

FOUR SPHERES

LICHT KUNST LICHT

As part of the 2007–8 roadshow organized by
Philips Lighting, this installation by Licht Kunst
Licht occupied one of the cargo containers given
over to the architects, designers and lighting
experts invited to unleash their creativity in
modulating space with light. The team, led by
Thomas Möritz, came up with a project, based
on one of his dreams, which, because its secret
could only be revealed through direct interaction,
relied on visitors' curiosity. Four light cannons,
each containing a cluster of narrow-beam LED
projectors, were directed onto red openings in
the centre of four suspended, mirror-polished
hemispheres. When inactive, red reflections
were produced, casting a dramatic glare over the
entire space. As soon as visitors began swinging
the hemispheres, they would immediately find
themselves in a futuristic version of a belfry, and
discover that, in reality, the light was all white.

YOU FADE TO LIGHT

RANDOM INTERNATIONAL

Design firm Random International, self-professed dedicated investigators into the 'direct and physical relationships' between the audience and the artwork, explores the potential of new lighting technologies. You Fade to Light creates a kinetic dialogue between the viewer and a grid of Lumiblade OLEDs, which at first appear as a faceted mirror. Bespoke software reflects the movements of the viewers, before they slowly dissolve into luminescence.

AMPLITUDE
RANDOM INTERNATIONAL

With this project, the creative team at Random International furthered its research into interactive light installations, in which added visual depth signifies a departure from the conventional idea of a flat, LED-based, low-resolution display towards a three-dimensional 'living sculpture'. Forty light arrays with 1,440 LEDs controlled by motion-tracking software were mounted perpendicular to the wall. 'The audience's movement now has the power to alter the spatial experience,' say the designers. Amplitude's large wall panels came alive with the dynamic light patterns and equally dynamic shadows that the installation casts on itself.

TRANSPOSITION
CUPPETELLI AND MENDOZA

Annica Cuppetelli and Cristobal Mendoza view their work as the continuation of the Kinetic and Op Art experiments in the twentieth century. Similarly focused on the exploration of light and vision, they draw upon digital technologies to create artworks in which real and virtual interact without direct contact. This installation is formed of a wall-mounted structure, in which hundreds of parallel elastic cords act as a projection screen for a digital animation featuring a similar number of lines. Participants' movements are captured by a camera and translated into virtual forces, which distort the computer-generated lines as if they were soft ropes, while the 'real' strings remain motionless. The result of a collaboration with Peter Segerstrom, the project is part of an ongoing series and completes the experience by adding an interactive sound component.

FLYLIGHT

STUDIO DRIFT

This interactive installation 'questions the delicate balance between the group and the individual,' note designers Lonneke Gordijn and Ralph Nauta. Flylight is an arrangement of glass tubes that light up in a seemingly unpredictable way, and mimics the self-organization of a flock, in which hundreds of birds move as a single entity, synchronizing speed and direction of flight and forming sophisticated patterns. Scientists have already discovered striking parallels in the behaviour of flocking birds and electrons in magnetized metals; the designers used custom-designed interactive software to translate the natural phenomenon into a meditative poetic gesture.

FUTURE SELF
RANDOM INTERNATIONAL

It is no surprise that choreographer Wayne McGregor, who is renowned for his cross-discipline collaborations, works extensively with Random International. The creative output of this London-based collective reveals a profound interest in human movement and spatial structures that engage in a dialogue with the moving body. In this installation, an assembly of LED-fitted brass rods confronts viewers with their full-length body image, translated into a three-dimensional formation of luminous points. In the minimalist tradition, the reflected image is reduced to the lowest resolution that it can still be recognized. A slight delay in the depiction adds an ethereal quality to the otherwise direct interaction.

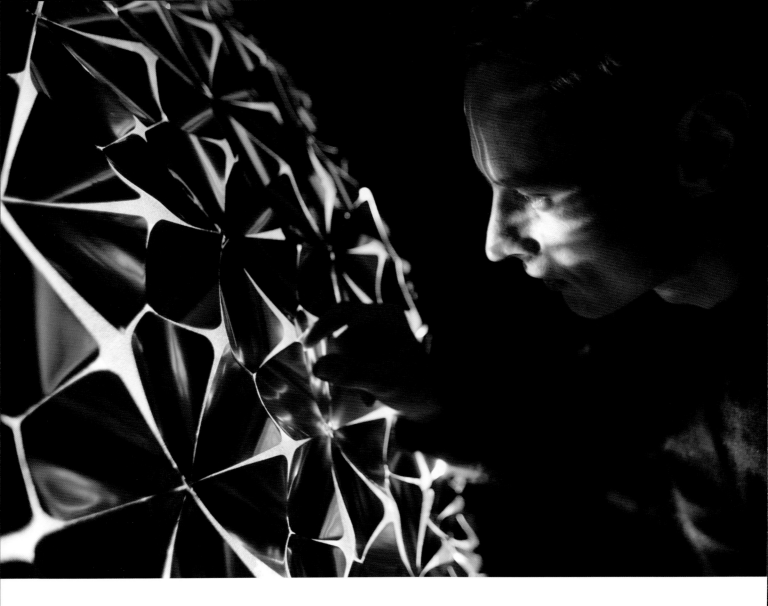

LOTUS DOME
STUDIO ROOSEGAARDE

In an interview for Lloyd Kahn's book
Domebook 2 in 1971, Buckminster Fuller
shared some thoughts on the possible
evolution of his geodesic dome. They
included the idea of a responsive outer skin,
whose cells could perform many functions:
'one could be a screen, others breathing
air, others letting light in, and the whole
thing could articulate just as sensitively as

a human being's skin.' Inspired by Fuller's
vision, Lotus Dome is composed of flower-
like elements made from heat-sensitive
aluminium foil. The project was exhibited
at the Sainte Marie-Madeleine church in
Lille, France. As the 'petals' unfurled when
touched, the light inside the dome became
increasingly visible, rendering the physical
walls of the structure nearly immaterial.

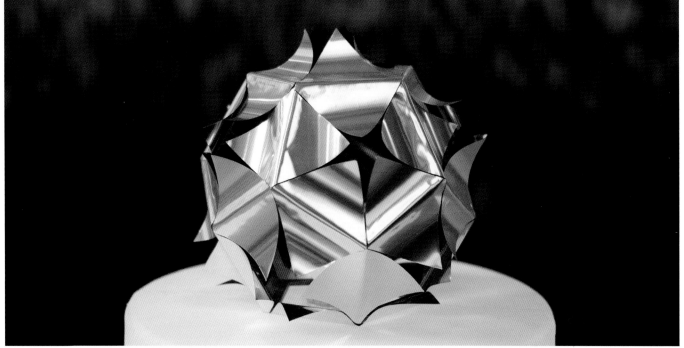

OVERTURE

TOSHIBA CORPORATION, TAKRAM DESIGN ENGINEERING,
RYO MATSUI

Toshiba produced Japan's first incandescent bulb in 1890; in 2008, the company set up the New Lighting Systems Division to focus on environmentally friendly light sources, paying special attention to the Japanese concept of *akari*, the capacity of light to appeal to our senses and emotions. The spirit of *akari* underpinned the installation designed by Tokyo firm Takram with architect Ryo Matsui to celebrate the launch of Toshiba's lighting business onto the European and US stage. Presented shortly before Europe began the phase-out of incandescent bulbs, the project reflected the paradigm shift in the world of lighting. Takram's design engineers placed LEDs into archetypal glass bulbs, half-filled with water and suspended at varying heights. Mirrors hung along the walls created the illusion of infinite arcades. The LEDs shone through the water, leaving circles of light on the sand-covered floor. Fitted with sensors, the subtly glimmering bulbs grew brighter when visitors came closer, and reacted to touch with a heartbeat-like pulsation.

SILO 468

HELSINKI, FINLAND
LIGHTING DESIGN COLLECTIVE

During Helsinki's reign as the World Design Capital in 2012, Madrid-based Lighting Design Collective won the competition for one of the city's headline projects, the conversion of a disused oil silo into a work of light art and a public space. The project marked the beginning of a massive urban redevelopment on the site of the former oil port, a highly visible coastal location in an area known for its strong winds. The wall was punctured with 2,012 holes and fitted with 1,280 white LEDs. The installation is activated through bespoke software based on swarm intelligence and nature-simulating algorithms that respond to the changing winds and other weather conditions. Refreshing every five minutes, the system generates fluid, never-repeating patterns, whose speed adjusts to that of the wind. Director Tapio Rosenius compares the installation to a living organism: the patterns themselves are not programmed, the designers just set the parameters that launch algorithms. The 16 m (52 ft 6 in.) high, self-ventilated interior space is painted deep red and animated with a mix of LED patterns and dappled reflections of the natural light provided by 450 polished steel mirrors.

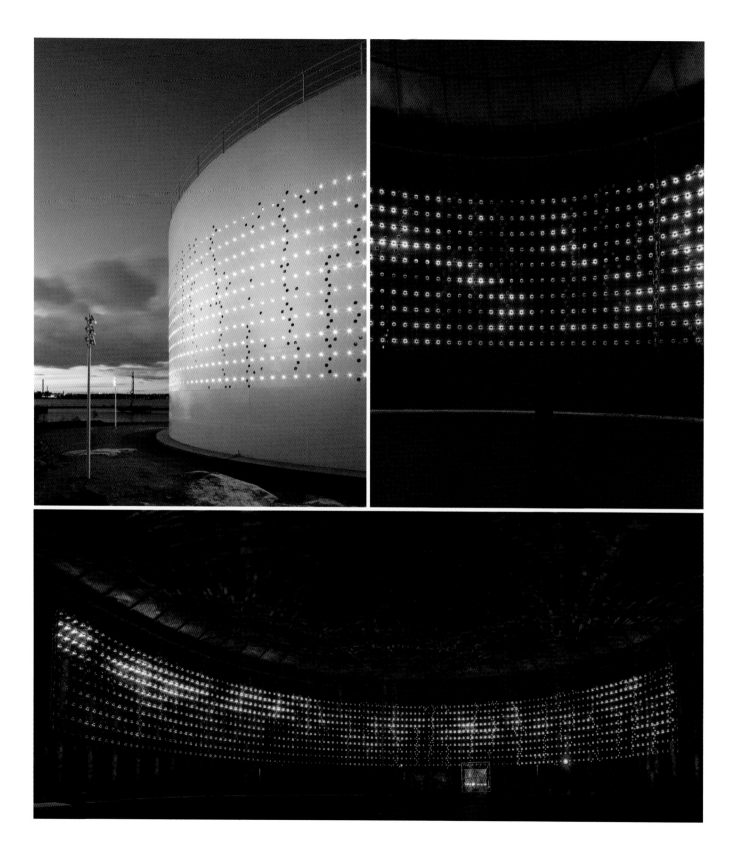

IMMERSION

A1 LOUNGE

VIENNA, AUSTRIA
EOOS

Multidisciplinary firm EOOS was tasked with designing an out-of-the-ordinary shopping experience for Mobilkom Austria. Back in 2004, when the project began, mobile telephony was relatively new and relevant store typologies had yet to be developed, along with ways of presenting the mix of physical and virtual products to customers. The team invented a series of new shopping rituals within an environment that combined 'high technology and archaic behaviours'. The entrance to the store was a key element of the design scheme. Following the example of novels and films, in which fog and backlighting signal the borderland between the familiar and the unknown, the team designed a 12 × 8 m (39 × 26 ft) glass façade with three fog machines sealed inside to produce billowing clouds of fog. The control system enabled different patterns of fog distribution throughout the day, with natural and artificial light filtered inside and outside the building. An illuminated glass floor enhances the otherworldly feel 'for human beings, for millions of years accustomed to light coming only from above'.

ATRIUM AT ME LONDON

LONDON, UK
FOSTER + PARTNERS

Regarded as the main spatial event of the ME London hotel, where everything, from the architecture to the bathroom fittings, was designed by Foster + Partners, the Radio Rooftop Bar is a toplit pyramidal space, soaring up to 24 m (80 ft) above the polished granite floor. The drama is heightened by the lighting scheme: natural light enters from above and indirect lighting delicately lines the perimeter of the floor, amplified by the white marble walls and highly reflective floor. Projected wall designs, in which marine creatures alternate with triangular patterns, further emphasize the scale of the space.

IN PASSING, REVOLVING DOORS
CHRIS FRASER

For In Passing (right and opposite), Chris Fraser created 'a multi-phased kinetic experience', in which visitors would walk through a custom-built corridor, pierced by large openings and narrow apertures. The corridor followed the perimeter of a gallery, with the red, green and blue light of the centrally suspended lamps producing 'interactive architectures'. In Revolving Doors (above), he employed a similar principle when designing a transitional space limited by centre-pivot doors that 'promised a measure of danger and play'.

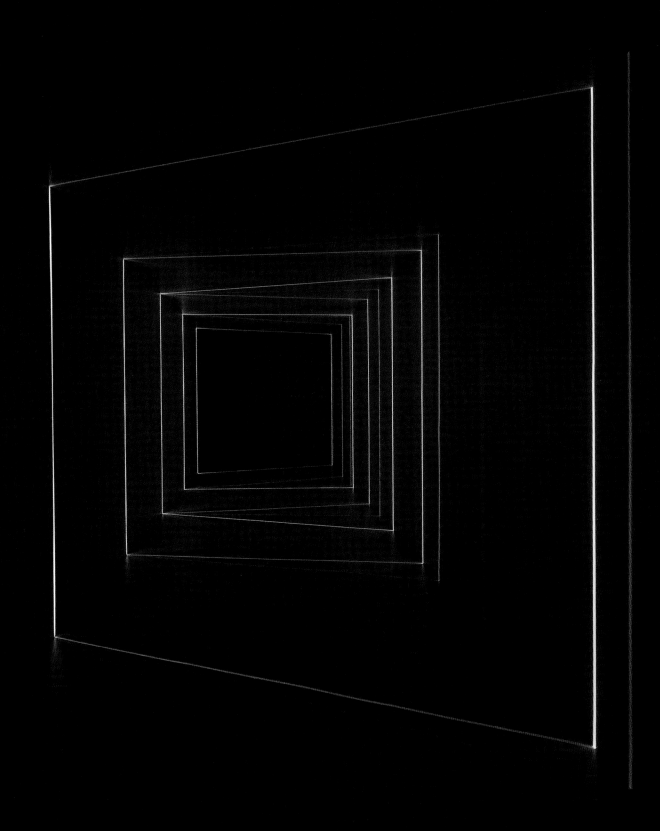

TWILIGHT

TOKUJIN YOSHIOKA

Like crepuscular rays that break through gaps in the clouds, Twilight floods the space with rays of light streaming through the white mist. Tokujin Yoshioka believes that senses and emotions can be designed, and proved this masterfully in this project for Italian furniture manufacturer Moroso. Presented during Milan Design Week 2011, a month after the disastrous earthquake and tsunami, it represented Yoshioka's meditations on the awe-inspiring force of nature and was an example of his creative desire to express the beauty of the natural world. The installation accompanied the premiere of the artist's new chair, whose shape, when seen from different angles, emulated the full and crescent moon. The milky light reflected off the surfaces of the chairs, allowing visitors to appreciate the textures of different kinds of white materials.

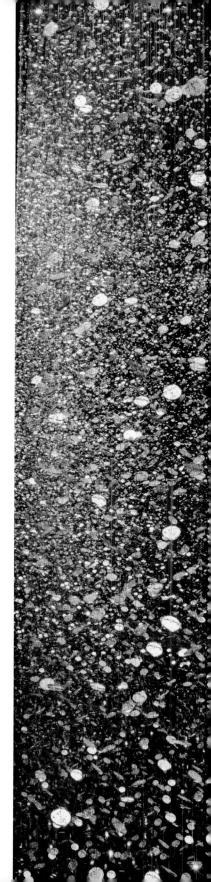

LIGHT IS TIME

DORELL GHOTMEH TANE

When Japanese watch brand Citizen asked
Paris-based architects Dan Dorell, Lina
Ghotmeh and Tsuyoshi Tane to design an
installation for Milan Design Week 2014, the
trio responded with a concept that fused the
watchmaking process with the cosmological
history of the universe. Suspended on thin
threads in a black space, thousands of watch
baseplates shimmered in the air – an effect
that looked like something between
the Big Bang and metallic rain – as a
representation of the origin of time and its
connection to light. Cut within this mass
of skilfully lit metallic discs were three
'clearings', in which the exhibits, from the
company's first pocket watch to its latest
satellite designs, were displayed.

SOUND CLOUD
KAZUHIRO YAMANAKA

When asked by experimental French firm Saazs to demonstrate the design potential of LEDinGLASS, Kazuhiro Yamanaka mounted sound modules onto light-emitting glass panels, turning them into luminous loudspeakers. The technology behind the material uses strips of coloured LEDs to direct a light beam through the edge of an extra-clear glass sheet. White enamelled dots covering the glass panel's front and rear sides reflect this light, producing a homogeneous diffused glow. With each panel consisting of three layers of glass, the designer took advantage of their structure to generate deep sound vibrations. A series of vertical panels were set across the space, inviting visitors to wander between them and enjoy the complex soundscape within.

TESSERACT

BORDEAUX, FRANCE
1024 ARCHITECTURE

The team at Paris-based 1024 Architecture used moving light in their interpretation of the mathematical concept of the four-dimensional cube: the tesseract. The installation consists of a cube-shaped scaffolding structure, which was wrapped in translucent fabric with robotic lights attached to it from the inside. Light beams form complex geometrical compositions, in which angles, depth and movement 'produce and deconstruct volumes in the air'. Tesseract was first presented at the New Forms Festival 2013 in Vancouver, Canada. Pictured here is the version displayed at the former submarine base in Bordeaux, France.

HANGING HOTEL

MASSIF DE L'ESTEREL, FRANCE
MARGOT KRASOJEVIC

Experimental architect Margot Krasojevic looks for new tools in the fields of neuroscience and psychology, among others, which define and alter our perception of space. Hanging Hotel, a projected rest stop for mountain climbers in southern France, uses some of these tools to provide its guests with both recreation and sensory adventures. The climbers' perceptions of the views outside and the immediate environment are conditioned by the hotel's architecture, specifically by the polarized glazing, which eliminates glare, and removable holographic filters used for the louvres that wrap around the pod-shaped rooms and provide shade, while heightening the viewing experience. Guests may choose between enjoying the 'real' picture, in which hallucinatory effects common to high altitudes are edited out by optical filters, or creating an alternative reality enabled by prismatic optical elements, which split sunlight into different colours that change with our angle of sight.

RAINBOW CHURCH
TOKUJIN YOSHIOKA

In his twenties, artist and designer Tokujin Yoshioka visited the Chapel of the Rosary in Vence, famously designed and decorated by Henri Matisse. Years later, he attempted to recreate that mystical experience of 'being filled with overwhelming light and vibrant colours' in his Rainbow Church installation.

The centrepiece of the project is a 12 m (40 ft)-high window that generates the effect of stained glass without a single coloured element. Instead, Yoshioka uses an assembly of 500 crystal prisms, which refract daylight into rainbow colours in a way that transforms the entire space.

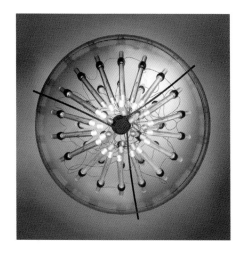

PROJECT CREDITS

LIGHT OBJECTS 001, 004, 006 [18]
Design and production: Naama Hofman
(naamahofman.com)

TRANSMISSION [19]
Design: Studio deFORM (studiodeform.com)
Production: Kavalierglass, Lasvit (lasvit.com)

MOBILE LAMP [20–1]
Luxembourg City, Luxembourg
Design: Nathalie Dewez (nathaliedewez.com)
Production: Airstar (airstar-light.com), Triline
Client: MUDAM

BLOCK [22]
Design: Johanna Jacobson Backman
(leverne.nu)
Production: Zero Lighting (zerolighting.com)

HOOD [23]
Design: Form Us With Love (formuswithlove.se)
Production: Ateljé Lyktan (atelje-lyktan.se)

D&D (DONNA & DONALD) [24]
Design and production: Ben Wirth (benwirth.de)

ASCENT [25]
Design: Daniel Rybakken (danielrybakken.com)
Production: Luceplan (luceplan.com)

SPILLO [26]
Design: Marco Pagnoncelli
Production: Icone (iconeluce.com)

FLASH [26]
Design and production: Davide Groppi
(davidegroppi.com)

NULLA [27]
Design and production: Davide Groppi
(davidegroppi.com)

IPNOS [27]
Design: Rossi Bianchi Lighting Design
(rossibianchi.com)
Production: Flos (flos.com)

**INTERNATIONAL TRIENNALE OF KOGEI
PRE-EVENT [28–9]**
Kanagawa, Japan
Design: Nendo (nendo.jp)

LIGHT [30]
Design: Yoy (yoy-idea.jp)

SHADE [30]
Design: Paul Cocksedge
(paulcocksedgestudio.com)
Production: Flos (flos.com)

TRANSPARENT LAMP [31]
Design: Nendo (nendo.jp)

MARBLE WITH FLUORESCENT TUBE [31]
Design: Brian Richer
Production: Castor Design (castordesign.ca)

SPYDER [32]
Design: Daast (daast.com.au)

ANYTIME [32]
Design: Alex Schulz (atschulzdesign.com)

YOGA CENTRE [33]
Beirut, Lebanon
Lighting design: .PSLAB (pslab.net)
Interior design: CBA Group (cbagrp.com)

STEREO KITCHEN [34–5]
Beirut, Lebanon
Lighting design: .PSLAB (pslab.net)
Interior design: Paul Kaloustian
(paulkaloustian.com)

ELAINE [1, 38]
Design: Daniel Becker (danielbecker.eu)
Production: Quasar (quasar.nl)

FRACTURE [38]
Design: Will Root (willrootdesign.com)

HOPE [39]
Design: Francisco Gomez Paz (gomezpaz.com),
Paolo Rizzatto (paolorizzatto.it)
Production: Luceplan (luceplan.com)

FRAGMENT [40]
Dubai, UAE
Design: United Visual Artists (uva.co.uk)
Client: Chalhoub Group

ADVENTURE [41]
Darlinghurst, Australia
Design: Korban Flaubert
(korbanflaubert.com.au)
Client: Object, Australian Design Centre

STARBRICK [42]
Design: Olafur Eliasson (olafureliasson.net)
Production: Zumtobel Lighting (zumtobel.com)

SNEAKEROLOGY [43]
Sydney, Australia
Design: Facet Studio (facetstudio.com.au)

SPACE FRAME [44]
Design: WHITEvoid (whitevoid.com)
Client: Vodafone

COLOR MANIFESTO [45]
Paris, France
Design: WHITEvoid (whitevoid.com)
Client: Renault

WALL PIERCING [46]
Design: Ron Gilad
Production: Flos (flos.com)

MONO-LIGHTS [47]
Design and production: OS&OOS
(osandoos.com)

GABRIEL CHANDELIER [48]
Versailles, France
Design: Ronan and Erwan Bouroullec
(bouroullec.com)
Client: Chateau de Versailles

LIVING SCULPTURE [49]
Design: WHITEvoid (whitevoid.com)
Client: Philips Lighting

BIT LIGHT [50]
Design and production: Choi + Shine Architects
(choishine.com)

*TRACK WALL [51]
Design and production: Ben Wirth (benwirth.de)

CLUSTER 2.0 [52]
Design and production: Ben Wirth (benwirth.de)

HYDRA [53]
Design: Carlotta de Bevilacqua

XL(AMP), XXXL(AMP) [56]
Design: Bart Lens (objetbart.be)
Production: Eden Design (edendesign.be)

CAPTURE [57]
Design: Paul Cocksedge
(paulcocksedgestudio.com)
Client: Friedman Benda gallery

24 LINES [58]
Montpellier, France
Design: 1024 Architecture
(1024architecture.net)
Client: La Panacée

STRING [59]
Design: Michael Anastassiades
(michaelanastassiades.com)
Production: Flos (flos.com)

UNDERGROUND SPA [60–1]
Limerick, Ireland
Design: Carmody Groarke (carmodygroarke.com)

ATLAS SPORTS CENTRE [62–3]
Paris, France
Design: Yoonseux Architectes (yoonseux.com)

EMG STONE GALLERY [64–5]
Guangzhou, China
Design: O-Office Architects (o-officearch.com)

DRAWING FASHION [66–7]
London, UK
Design: Carmody Groarke
(carmodygroarke.com), A Practice For Everyday
Life (apracticeforeverydaylife.com)
Client: Design Museum

WALL CLOUD [68–9]
Tokyo, Japan
Interior design: Sasaki Associates
(ryuichisasaki.com)
Lighting design: CHIPS LLC (chipsss.com),
Lighting Sou (lighting-sou.com)

WHITE GEOLOGY [70–1]
Paris, France
Design: Philippe Rahm (philipperahm.com)
Client: Centre National des Arts Plastiques,
Réunion des Musées Nationaux, Ministère
de la Culture

DOMESTIC ASTRONOMY [72–3]
Humlebæk, Denmark
Design: Philippe Rahm (philipperahm.com)
Client: Louisiana Museum of Modern Art

HANGING FOREST [76–7]
Brussels, Belgium
Design: Gilbert Moity (gilbertmoity.com)
Client: Patrick Roger

SOCIAL CLUB [78]
Paris, France
Design: 1024 Architecture
(1024architecture.net)

UCHI LOUNGE 01 [79]
Sydney, Australia
Design: Facet Studio (facetstudio.com.au)

ZOLLVEREIN GALLERY COAL WASHER [80–1]
Essen, Germany
Design: OMA (oma.eu), Heinrich Böll
(architekt-boell.de)
Lighting design: Licht Kunst Licht
(lichtkunstlicht.com)

ST BOTOLPH BUILDING [82–3]
London, UK
Design: Grimshaw Architects
(grimshaw-architects.com)
Lighting design: Speirs + Major
(speirsandmajor.com)

ONE BEAM OF LIGHT [84]
London, UK
Design: GNI Projects (gni-projects.com)
Client: Light Collective and Concord Sylvania

POSITION – N 46°38'47" E 14°53'31" [85]
Neuhaus, Austria
Design: Querkraft Architekten (querkraft.at)
Artwork: Brigitte Kowanz (kowanz.com)
Client: Museum Liaunig

**PARIS 8 UNIVERSITY ARTS DEPARTMENT
[86–7]**
Saint-Denis, France
Design: Moussafir Architectes (moussafir.fr),
Bernard Dufournet

PRENZLAUER BERG RESIDENCE [90]
Berlin, Germany
Design: Wolff Architekten (wolffarchitekten.com)
Production: Lucem (lucem.de)

BANK OF GEORGIA [90–1]
Tbilisi, Georgia
Design: Dephani (dephani.com)
Production: Lucem (lucem.de)

YII EXHIBITION [92]
Design: Nendo (nendo.jp)
Client: National Taiwan Craft Research Institute

WALLOVER, FLYING DOTS [93]
Design (Wallover): Tomas Erel
Design (Flying Dots): Christian Biecher
(biecher.com)
Production: Saazs (saazs.com)

LOGAN OFFICE [94–5]
New York, New York
Design: SO-IL (so-il.org)

AUDITORIUM [96]
Design: Paul Cocksedge
(paulcocksedgestudio.com)
Client: 100% Design

LIGHT SEGMENTS SPACE [97]
Artist: Kimchi and Chips (kimchiandchips.com)

LE CIEL BLEU [98–9]
Osaka, Japan
Design: Noriyuki Otsuka (nodo.jp)
Lighting consultant: Kenjiro Ikeda

**YOU AND I HORIZONTAL, BETWEEN YOU AND I,
FIVE MINUTES OF PURE SCULPTURE [100–1]**
Artist: Anthony McCall (anthonymccall.com)

ARCADES [102–3]
Artist: Troika (troika.uk.com)

LEXUS L-FINESSE [104–5]
Design: Tokujin Yoshioka (tokujin.com)
Client: Lexus

VANISHING POINT [106–7]
Artist: United Visual Artists (uva.co.uk)
Client: Towner Gallery

SHONAN CHRIST CHURCH [114–15]
Kanagawa, Japan
Design: Takeshi Hosaka (hosakatakeshi.com)
Engineering consultants: Arup (arup.com)

KORO HOUSE [116–17]
Toyota, Japan
Design: Katsutoshi Sasaki
(sasaki-as.com)

HOUSE IN KOMAE [118–19]
Tokyo, Japan
Lighting design: Makoto Yamaguchi (ymgci.net),
Mayumi Kondo

DAYLIGHT HOUSE [120–1]
Tokyo, Japan
Design: Takeshi Hosaka (hosakatakeshi.com)

CLYFFORD STILL MUSEUM [122–3]
Denver, Colorado
Design: Allied Works Architecture
(alliedworks.com)
Lighting consultant: Arup (arup.com)

UNDERHOUSE [124]
Yvelines, France
Design: Paul Coudamy

STÄDEL MUSEUM [125]
Frankfurt, Germany
Design: Schneider + Shumacher
(schneider-schumacher.de), Licht Kunst Licht
(lichtkunstlicht.com)

DAYLIGHT ENTRANCE,
SUBCONSCIOUS EFFECTS OF DAYLIGHT,
DAYLIGHT COMES SIDEWAYS [126–7]
Design: Daniel Rybakken
Client (Daylight Entrance): Vasakronan AB

WHITE LIGHT [128]
Design: Paul Cocksedge
(paulcocksedgestudio.com)
Client: Friedman Benda

COELUX [129]
Design: Paolo Di Trapani
Production: CoeLux (coelux.com)

DEVELOPING A MUTABLE HORIZON,
ONE LINE DRAWING [132–3]
Design: Chris Fraser

MELT AND RECREATE [134]
Design: Siri Bahlenberg (siriba.com),
Sofia Bergfeldt (sofiabergfeldt.com)

SWELL [135]
Design: Paul Cocksedge
(paulcocksedgestudio.com)
Production: Yamagiwa (yamagiwa.co.jp)

SURFACE TENSION LAMP [1, 135]
Design: Front (frontdesign.se)
Collaborator: Loligo

LIGHT IN WATER [136–7]
Design: Dorell Ghotmeh Tane
(dgtarchitects.com)
Lighting design: Izumi Okayasu (ismidesign.com)

WATER LAMPS [11, 138]
Design: Arturo Erbsman (arturoerbsman.com)

DAY & NIGHT LIGHT [139]
Design: Éléonore Delisse (eleonoredelisse.com)

HAFENCITY UNIVERSITÄT STATION [140–1]
Hamburg, Germany
Architect: Raupach Architekten
(raupach-architekten.de)
Container design: Stauss + Pedrazzini
Lighting design: Pfarré Lighting Design
(lichtplanung.com), d-lightvision
(d-lightvision.de)
Client: Hamburger Hochbahn AG

SPECTRAL APARTMENT [142–3]
Levallois, France
Design: Nicolas Dorval-Bory (nicolasdorvalbory.
fr), Raphaël Bétillon (raphaelbetillon.fr)

RAINBOW STATION [144–5]
Amsterdam, Netherlands
Design: Studio Roosegaarde
(studioroosegaarde.net)

FREE PIXEL [148]
Design: Carlo Ratti (carloratti.com)
Client: Artemide (artemide.com)

VECTOR [149]
Courbevoie, France
Design: Trafik (lavitrinedetrafik.fr)
Production: Saazs (saazsblog.com)
Client: French Patent Office

MULTIVERSE [150–1]
Washington, DC
Artist: Leo Villareal (villareal.net)
Client: National Gallery of Art

DIURNISME [152]
Paris, France
Design: Philippe Rahm (philipperahm.com)

SPLIT TIMES CAFÉ [153]
Leibling, Austria
Design: Philippe Rahm (philipperahm.com)
Client: FOC Eybesfeld

BLUE SKY LAMP [154]
Design: Chris Kabel (chriskabel.com)
PHASES, LUNAIRE [155]
Design: Ferréol Babin (ferreolbabin.fr)
Production (Lunaire): Fontana Arte
(fontanaarte.com)

SYZYGY SERIES [156]
Design and production: OS&OOS
(osandoos.com)

THANKS FOR THE SUN,
THANKS FOR THE PLANETS [157, 253]
Design and production: Arnout Meijer
(arnoutmeijer.nl)

MOMENTUM [158–9]
London, UK
Design: United Visual Artists (uva.co.uk)
Client: The Curve, Barbican Centre

SHADE [160–1]
London, UK
Design and production: Simon Heijdens
(simonheijdens.com)
Client: The Art Institute of Chicago

ENDLESS [161]
Design: Bram Vanderbeke
(bramvanderbeke.com)

RIPPLE [162]
Design: Poetic Lab (poetic-lab.com)
Production: J. & L. Lobmeyr (lobmeyr.at)

POLARIS, LOUMINOUS ALCHEMY [162–3]
Design: Laurent Fort (customartlight.com)

MOBILE CHANDELIERS [170, 255]
Design and production: Michael Anastassiades
Studio (michaelanastassiades.com)

IPPARCO [210]
Design: Neil Poulton (neilpoulton.com)
Production: Artemide (artemide.com)

PULL OVER [211]
Design: Bina Baitel (binabaitel.com)
Supported by VIA 2008 (via.fr)

FRAGMENT [211]
Design: Ferréol Babin (ferreolbabin.fr)

ALONE AT WORK [212]
Design and production: Regent Lighting
(regent.ch)

SUSTAINABLE DANCE FLOOR [213]
Design: Studio Roosegaarde
(studioroosegaarde.net)
Client: Sustainable Dance Club

DISCO DISCO [214–5]
Design and production: Alex Asseily,
Haberdashery (haberdasherylondon.com)

FOUR SPHERES [216]
Design: Licht Kunst Licht (lichtkunstlicht.com)
Client: Philips Lighting

YOU FADE TO LIGHT [217]
Design: Random International
(random-international.com)

AMPLITUDE [218]
Design: Random International
(random-international.com)

TRANSPOSITION [219]
Design: Cuppetelli and Mendoza
(cuppetellimendoza.com)
Collaborator: Peter Segerstrom (flatflat.org)

FLYLIGHT [220]
Design: Studio Drift (studiodrift.com)

FUTURE SELF [221]
Design: Random International
(random-international.com)

LOTUS DOME [222–3]
Design: Studio Roosegaarde
(studioroosegaarde.net)

OVERTURE [224–5]
Design: Toshiba Corporation (toshiba.co.jp),
Takram Design Engineering (takram.com),
Ryo Matsui (matsui-architects.com)
Client: Toshiba Corporation

SILO 468 [226–7]
Helsinki, Finland
Design: Lighting Design Collective (ldcol.com)

A1 LOUNGE [230–1]
Vienna, Austria
Design: EOOS (eoos.com)
Client: Mobilkom Austria

ATRIUM AT ME LONDON [232–3]
London, UK
Design: Foster + Partners
(fosterandpartners.com)

IN PASSING, REVOLVING DOORS [234–5]
Design: Chris Fraser (chrisfraserstudio.com)
Client (In Passing): Disjecta Contemporary
Art Center
Client (Revolving Doors): SF Camerawork

TWILIGHT [236–7]
Design: Tokujin Yoshioka (tokujin.com)
Client: Moroso

LIGHT IS TIME [238–9]
Design: Dorell Ghotmeh Tane
(dgtarchitects.com)
Client: Citizen

SOUND CLOUD [240]
Design: Kazuhiro Yamanaka
(kazuhiroyamanaka.com)
Production: SAAZS (saazsblog.com)

TESSERACT [241]
Bordeaux, France
Design: 1024 Architecture
(1024architecture.net)

HANGING HOTEL [242–3]
Massif de l'Esterel, France
Design: Margot Krasojevic
(margotkrasojevic.org)
Client: HoldenManz Wine Estate

RAINBOW CHURCH [244–5]
Design: Tokujin Yoshioka (tokujin.com)

RELUMINE NO.6/30 [256]
Design: mischer'traxler Studio
(mischertraxler.com)

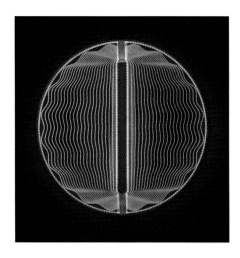

DESIGNERS

ARTISTS

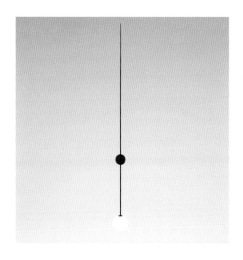

PHOTO CREDITS

1 (left), **135** (right) Pär Olofsson; **9** Fulvio Orsenigo © 2015 Doug Wheeler; courtesy David Zwirner, New York/London; **11** (top left) Tom Vack; (top right) © 2013 Konica Minolta, Inc. **18** (top left) Rami Salomon; (top right) Dan Perez; (bottom right) Yael Engelhart; **19** (top and bottom right) Martin Chum; **20–1** Stijn Bollaert; **25** (top left) Luceplan; **25** (top right and bottom), **126**, **127** (top left), **199**, **210** (left) Kalle Sanner and Daniel Rybakken; **27** (right) Leo Torri; **28–9**, **118–19** Daici Ano; **30** (left) Yasuko Furukawa; **31** (left) Masayuki Hayashi; **32** (left) Rodrick Bond; **33** .PSLAB; **34–5** Joe Kesrouani; **39** (top and bottom right) Tom Vack; (bottom left) Santi Caleca; **41** Andrew Stevens; **42** (top) Jens Ziehe/Zumtobel Lighting © 2009 Olafur Eliasson; (bottom) Studio Olafur Eliasson/Zumtobel Lighting © 2009 Olafur Eliasson; **43** Katherine Lu; **44–5**, **49** Christopher Bauder; **46** (left), **129** (top and bottom right) Michael Loos; **51** Simone Naumann; **52** Robert Pupeter; **57**, **96**, **128** Mark Cocksedge; **58**, **78** Brice Pelleschi; **60–1**

Christian Richters; **62–3** Alexandra Mocanu; **64–5** Likyfoto; **66–7** Richard Davies; **68–9** Takumi Ota; **72–3** Brøndum & Co; **76–7** John Picat; **79** Andrew Chung; **80**, **81** (top) Thomas Mayer; **81** (bottom, left and right) Licht Kunst Licht/Luc Bernard; **82–3** James Newton; **85** Lisa Rastl; **86** (top), **87** (right, middle and bottom) Mario Palmieri; **87** (left and top right) Georges Fessy; **87** (bottom) Claire Petetin; **93** (top) Eric Traoré; (bottom, left and right) Morgane Le Gall; **94–5** Iwan Baan; **98–9** Hiroyuki Hirai; **100** (left), **101** Blaise Adilon; courtesy Sprüth Magers Berlin London; **100** (right) Sean Gallup/Getty Images; courtesy Sprüth Magers Berlin London; **105**, **245** Nacása & Partners, Inc.; **114–15**, **120–1** Koji Fujii/Nacása & Partners, Inc.; **122–3** Jeremy Bittermann; **125** Norbert Miguletz Fotografie; **127** (top right, bottom left and right) Daniel Rybakken; **136–7**, **238–9** Takuji Shimmura; **139** Laurids Gallée; **140–1** Markus Tollhopf; **149** Pascal Nottoli; **150–1** courtesy Sandra Gering, Inc., New York, NY; **152** Adam Rzepka, Centre Pompidou; **157**, **253** (top) Pim Top;

(bottom) Arnout Meijer Studio; **158–9** United Visual Artists/James Medcraft; **160** Charles Emerton; **172** Tom Vack © Ingo Maurer GmbH, Munich; **174–5** Mirjam Bleeker; **176**, **177** (top left and middle right) Karel Duerinckx; **177** (bottom right) Tim Meier; **181** Kozo Takayama; **183** Hisao Suzuki; **185** Takeshi Asano; Shizuka Takahashi; **186** (top) Felipe Ribon; (bottom) Fred Fiol; **187** Mark C. O'Flaherty; **194** Torben Eskerod; **196** Stephen Iles; **198** Marco Canevacci; Simone Serlenga; **202** (left and bottom right) Laetitia Bica; **211** (left) Marie Flores; **216** (top) Licht Kunst Licht/Thomas Möritz; (bottom) Philips; **217** (bottom) Some/Things; **218** James Harris; **220** (bottom) Adrien Millot; **224–5** Daici Ano © 2012 Toshiba Corporation; **226**, **227** (top left) Tuomas Uusheimo; **227** (top right) Tapio Rosenius; (bottom) Hannu Iso-oja; **230**, **231** (bottom right) Bruno Klomfar; **231** (top and bottom left) Hans-Georg Esch; **232** MF London; **233** Nigel Young/Foster + Partners; **234** (top) Benjamin Hoffman; **241** Emmanuel Gabily

To Therina and Löwka

On the cover: *Front* Rainbow Church, Tokujin Yoshioka; *back,
top row, left to right*; Revolving Doors, Chris Fraser; Transmission,
Studio deFORM; XL(amp), Bart Lens; *middle row, left to right*
Spectral Apartment, Nicolas Dorval-Bory and Raphaël Bétillon;
Disco Disco, Alex Asseily and Haberdashery; Daylight House,
Takeshi Hosaka; *bottom row, left to right* One Line Drawing,
Chris Fraser; Elaine, Daniel Becker; Day & Night Light,
Éléonore Delisse

Lumitecture: Illuminating Interiors for Designers and Architects
© 2016 Anna Yudina

Designed by Anna Yudina

First published in 2016 in hardcover in the United States of
America by Thames & Hudson Inc., 500 Fifth Avenue, New York,
New York 10110

thamesandhudsonusa.com

Library of Congress Catalog Card Number 2015943659

ISBN 978-0-500-51834-2

Printed in China by Shanghai Offset Printing Products Limited

RELUMINE NO.6/30
MISCHER'TRAXLER STUDIO

For this limited-edition series, Katharina Mischer
and Thomas Traxler of Vienna-based studio
mischer'traxler find new uses for old lamps by
creatively updating their light sources. Each
item from the Relumine collection is created by
thoroughly revamping two discarded lamps and
merging them into a single piece with the help of
a new-generation fluorescent tube.

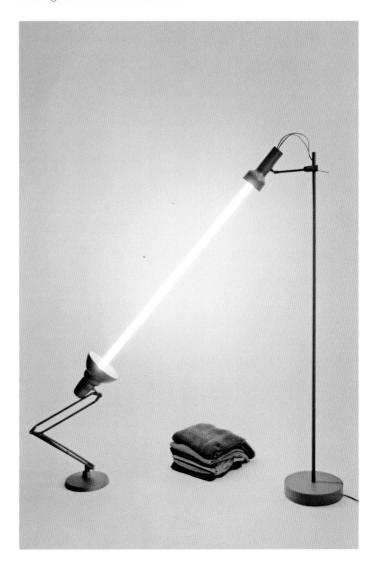